CONVERSATION PIECES

J. S. Copley   *Reproduced by gracious permission of H.M. the King*

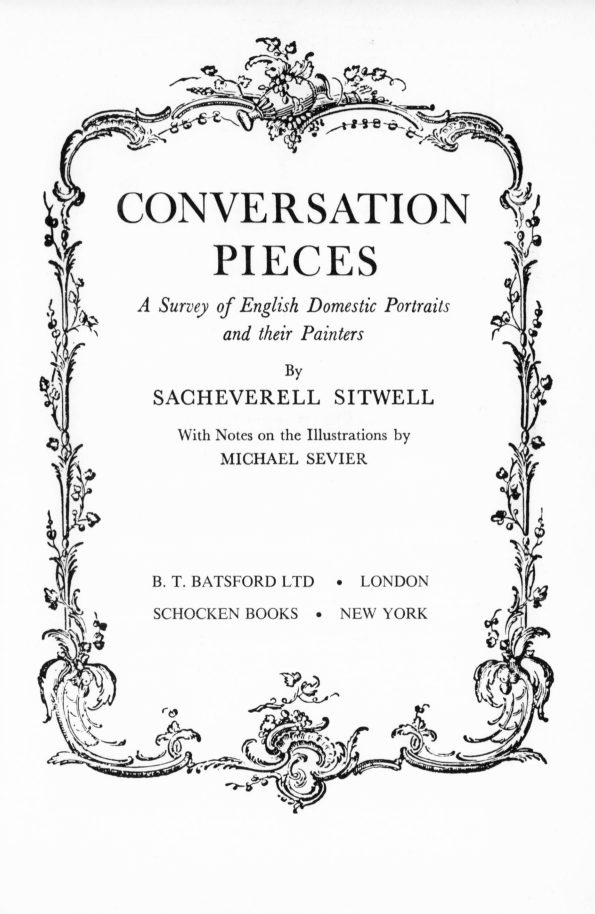

CONVERSATION PIECES

*A Survey of English Domestic Portraits
and their Painters*

By

SACHEVERELL SITWELL

With Notes on the Illustrations by

MICHAEL SEVIER

B. T. BATSFORD LTD • LONDON

SCHOCKEN BOOKS • NEW YORK

This volume is a faithful reproduction of the first printing, Batsford, 1936,
with the exception that the colour plates have been reproduced in monochrome.

First published in this format in 1969 by
B. T. Batsford Ltd
4 Fitzhardinge Street, London W 1

and

Schocken Books Inc.
67 Park Avenue, New York, N.Y. 10016

Library of Congress Catalog Card No. 69-19622

Manufactured in the United States of America

To

THE RIGHT HON. SIR PHILIP SASSOON, BART.

M.P., G.B.E., C.M.G.

TO WHOM THE CONVERSATION PIECE,

AND ZOFFANY, MORE ESPECIALLY,

ARE DEEPLY INDEBTED

CONTENTS

PREFACE

In writing this book the author has been under repeated obligation to Dr. G. C. Williamson, his predecessor in the same field, and a friend from childhood. *John Zoffany, R.A.* (written in collaboration with Lady Victoria Manners), and his *English Conversation Pictures* are full of information and have had to be consulted on innumerable occasions throughout the preparation of this book. All owners of the pictures illustrated must be thanked, individually and collectively, for their kind services in allowing reproductions to be made; while a special note of thanks is due, more particularly, to Sir Alec Martin, Sir Herbert Hughes-Stanton, R.A., Sir Robert Witt, Mr. Felix Harbord, Messrs. Knoedler, Tooth, Leger, and Leggatt, Mr. Arthur de Casseres and Mr. Oliver Brown, who have rendered invaluable assistance. Thanks are also due to the Proprietors of *Punch* for permission to include the Du Maurier cartoon reproduced on page 87. Finally, the author would like to express his obligations to Mr. Michael Sevier, who has worked indefatigably upon the notes and the illustrations, and to Mr. Charles Fry, who has been the inspirer and the force of energy behind this most pleasant of tasks.

SACHEVERELL SITWELL.

November, 1936.

NOTE

FOR this reissue of *Conversation Pieces* it should be noted that the birth of Zoffany is now established as having taken place at Ratisbon in 1725 and not at Frankfurt in 1733. Furthermore, it becomes increasingly apparent that much critical work still remains to be done upon Zoffany, and that many pictures loosely attributed to him may be in reality by other as yet little known painters of the school.

A few wrong attributions and small errors pointed out by reviewers and others have been corrected.

CONVERSATION PIECES

2. From Heideloff's *Gallery of Fashion*, January, 1799

3. THE ARTIST, HIS WIFE AND CHILD

Thomas Gainsborough

Sir Philip Sassoon, Bart.

CHAPTER I

INTRODUCTION

THERE are certain qualities of the English genius which find their expression in the English Conversation Piece. If a considerable body of these paintings are collected together their emergence as a school can be definitely established. But the first problem that is posed to a writer upon the Conversation Piece is what to include and what to omit. The limits must be defined as strictly as possible before the discussion begins.

It is not possible, for instance, to include Hogarth's Marriage à la Mode or The March to Finchley as Conversation Pieces. Neither, on the other hand, are the numerous and excellent pictures by Zoffany of theatrical scenes within our province. In each case, it is another genre of painting, and not the Conversation Piece. Nor can the sporting picture find a place in this category, for it, also, is a branch of art to itself. This deprives us of a great many paintings by Stubbs, and of Ben Marshall, Herring, and many more. At the same time, pictures by Morland and Walton must be excluded. They, too, are paintings of genre and not Conversation Pieces. It is clear, then, that the necessity is for a picture to portray definite personalities in their intimate surroundings. A single portrait cannot make a Conversation Piece.

But, also, the size of the picture is a criterion by which to judge it. Modest dimensions must be insisted upon; or else the huge painting of the Beaumont family by Romney, in the National Gallery, will become one of the chief works of the school. On the other hand, the Conversation Piece may, legitimately, be diminished in scale so as to include drawings, silhouettes, or even book illustrations. This is because they adhere strictly to the necessary principles. They are Conversation Pieces, in little.

Perhaps the most easy method by which its correct properties can be defined is by tracing back the conversation picture to its earliest known examples. The primitives of the school should contain the foreshadowing of its future successes. A picture which is nearly, but not quite, a Conversation Piece is a painting of Sir Peter Lely and his family, in the possession of Viscount Lee of Fareham (4). It might be described as a mingling of Van Dyck and the Dutch school. The left hand part of the picture, which is a concert of music, betrays an influence of Adrian Brouwer; while the

I

true interest of the painting, which centres in the four simultaneous figures of his wife, clothed and unclothed, is conspicuous for its suggestion of Van Dyck. The third portrait, with her naked back to the spectator, introduces a third element of mythology. She is offering a cup to the seated Venus and her attendant maiden; so that the painting is, at once, a genre picture, a mythological scene, and a group of portraits. It can scarcely, therefore, be termed a Conversation Piece. This is the Dutch, or Flemish, genius not yet acclimatized to our shores.

The age of Charles II, of Grinling Gibbons and the red brick architecture of Wren, is the assertion of this influence from Holland. It appears in every detail of domestic architecture, in doors and mantelpieces and in the silver of the time. The reign of the Dutchman, William III, came in confirmation of this. The trend of taste was away from the French or Italian style and towards the Dutch. Hampton Court is in illustration of this principle; and yet its results are purely of this island. For there is nothing more typical of England than Hampton Court. This is because, through the genius of Wren, the Dutch predominance has been digested and controlled.

The perfect reflection of this period of transition is in a picture that is reproduced herewith (5). Its author is Henry Danckerts, a Dutchman from The Hague who studied in Italy and was invited to England by Charles II. He was employed by the King in painting views of the Royal Palaces and of the sea ports of England and Wales; more particularly of that latter country, we are mysteriously told. No fewer than twenty-eight of his landscapes and views were in the collection of James II.

The present picture, which may have been unique in his production, represents Mr. Rose, the Royal gardener, presenting the first pineapple ever grown in England to Charles II. This painting was, later, in the possession of Horace Walpole, and at least two replicas are known. In the background is Dawnay Court, Surrey, which belonged to Charles II. The King is standing upon some steps which are a landing stage to the Thames, while we are told, in parenthesis, that the ancient pine pits existed in this garden till as recently as 1929.

The likeness of the King is extraordinarily good, as can be tested by a visit to his waxwork figure in Westminster Abbey. He is shown as very tall and very Spanish, or Hapsburg, in type, there being a close resemblance to his cousin, the Emperor Leopold I of Austria. The formal pattern of the parterres in the background and the arrangement of terracotta pots round the fountain brim are in harmony with the trim formality of that Carolean house. It is probable that this is the most natural portrait of Charles II

2

Sir Peter Lely

4. THE FAMILY OF THE ARTIST

Viscount Lee of Fareham

5. "THE PINEAPPLE PICTURE"

Henry Danckerts   *Sir Philip Sassoon, Bart.*

6. Trade Card engraved by Hogarth for his Sister

ever taken; and every circumstance and association of this painting lifts it, as it were, into a little niche or compartment to itself. It possesses to a marked degree the sufficiency of the Conversation Piece, which must have an existence to itself as the unfolding of some anecdote or situation. This picture, then, is an early Conversation Piece dating from a century, or more, before the perfection of the style.

In its origin the Conversation Piece is of Dutch provenance. The intimacies of de Hoogh, of Metsu and Mieris are translated into terms of portraiture and character. It was not the still life that interested the Englishmen, but the similitude to living people. The formal portrait by Lely or Kneller, which was based upon Van Dyck, could not possess this truth of appearances. But it required the more lively talents of a Hogarth to create the school. Hogarth and Zoffany are its chief ornaments. In their hands the still realities of the Dutchmen turned to living characters. The scene, moreover, was lifted from the tavern, or from the parlour giving on to the canal and, instead, we are shown the Georgian interior. If it be Hogarth, we have the Handelian architecture of Gibbs; or, with Zoffany, the setting is an Adam room, or the sylvan glades of a park. The Conversation Piece has become English and no longer Dutch.

Once this has been achieved, the pictures multiply and attempt every ramification that is open to them. We have not only the Conversation Piece proper but a period of indetermination in which the landscape and the sporting picture, two other styles in which the English painter was to excel, are undecided as to their respective properties and take on the habiliments of each other. Two plates are given here in which John Wootton, the first of our equine painters, has represented Lady Beauchamp and Lady Rivers in what could be described as a conversation of horses and carriages (8), and some members of the Beaufort Hunt, on foot or on horseback, but in the stillness of the library or study (7).

If we may leave the Conversation Piece, for the moment, in the hands of Hogarth or Zoffany, who will receive every attention in the two ensuing chapters, there will be space to deal among these preliminaries with many lesser things that might escape attention, but should be an essential part of this context. For the properties of the Conversation Piece, as established by Hogarth and Zoffany, descended into many minor or secondary things and, from the sum of these, it should be possible to state the full properties of our subject and the points in which its excellence consists.

There could, for example, be no better specimens of the Conversation Piece than the two silhouettes with which this book is illustrated. These are painted with Indian ink on paper and are the work of an unknown

The Sitwell and Warneford Families, about 1776.   A Silhouette by Torond in
the collection of Osbert Sitwell, Esq.

artist, Torond, of French and probably Huguenot extraction. This forgotten
person must have been the supreme master of his art of silhouette. His
shadow pictures possess the qualities of a Beardsley drawing, to which,
indeed, they have an actual resemblance, as can be seen in the table on the
left hand side of the smaller of the two silhouettes. This is exactly in the

'A Birthday Party': a Silhouette Group by Torond, now in the Victoria
and Albert Museum.   *Circa* 1785.

style of Beardsley. It must have been a limited field in which Torond could express his talents. The laws of profile had to be observed, as in Egyptian or Etruscan painting. Only certain accessories were suitable, and these had to come into use again and again. Incidentally, the same Hepplewhite chairs and an identical openwork basket appear in both drawings, as if the artist had insisted upon these excuses for his sleight of hand. It is certain that other mannerisms would be observable were more works by Torond available to study, for the silhouette is the most mannered and limited of mediums. A glance, though, at the silhouettes of lesser masters in this medium, such as Wellings, will serve to establish the perfection of these two examples, which are comparable to a beautiful stage scene prolonged by a miracle in time and to be closed, perhaps, as in the larger of the two drawings, by the falling of the curtain.

There are many silhouettes of this earlier period, and of the 'twenties and 'thirties, that are among the lesser ornaments of the Conversation Piece. But the immensity of its scope must include, also, such typical works of their kind as some of the groups from Nicholas Heideloff's *Gallery of Fashion*. This publication was begun, in monthly parts, in 1794 and continued till 1803. It is, with the exception of *Le Monument de Costume*, the most sumptuous fashion magazine ever produced. But its plates, unlike those of Moreau le Jeune, have the advantage of hand colouring while the ornaments are done in gold and silver and in metallic shades of green and copper. Their author, Heideloff, was a German from Stuttgart who worked in Paris and fled to London on the outbreak of the Revolution. The plates are the work, exclusively, of Heideloff and certain of their number, of which we reproduce a selection, are perfect models of their kind.

The drawing of two young ladies driving a pair of white horses in a high gig or phaeton is a particularly exciting example of his powers (9). Perhaps it gains in drama by the height of their position and the curbed speed of the horses. And the lines of the harness are applied in silver, which imparts to this delicate drawing something of the quality of a suri-mono by Hokusai or Utamaro. There are others, no less bold in design and exquisite in finish. Two ladies, for instance, seated at a table on which there stands a silver tea urn, rendered in that same technique, while a splendid Adam carpet unrolls its flowers and emblems beneath their feet (2). Or another, which is a little family group in the open air. In this, the young boy in a red suit and his sister and mother can be compared to a Zoffany or Copley. The elegant simplicity of the Directoire period is given expression in inimitable manner in these drawings, so that this rare book is a culmination of the whole eighteenth century. Who would think, on looking at these plates, that the crinoline and the bustle were still to come? There is the foretaste of modern or contemporary dress in the designs of Heideloff. The encumbered and unhygienic stresses of the mid-Victorian age seem like a wild improbability coming after the *Gallery of Fashion*.

From Moses' *Modern Costume* (1823).

The succeeding age of the Regency, or Classical revived, is to be seen portrayed in an unique book of engravings by Henry Moses, which work is no less important as a document of its age. The engraver was a young artist who was given employment by Henry Hope, the collector. This personage, a kind of secondary Beckford, is responsible for some of the finest examples of Regency furniture made for his house at Deepdene, near Dorking, from his own designs, or to those of Percier and Fontaine whom he employed. Hope worked, also, upon books, depicting the dress and furniture of classical times. It was in this connection that Moses was engaged by him; but in subsequent works executed on his own initiative the influence of Hope is no less apparent. The book that is under

From Moses' *Modern Costume* (1823).

discussion is an instance of this. The engravings are done with so fine a point that the work becomes like cameo or intaglio cutting. Not only are they

6

7. MEMBERS OF THE BEAUFORT HUNT

John Wootton *Tate Gallery, London*

8. THE BEAUCHAMP AND RIVERS FAMILIES, AND SIR NEVILLE HICKMAN

John Wootton

9.   From Heideloff's *Gallery of Fashion*, August, 1794

of interest because of their place in the history of taste, but their fineness and delicacy of execution put them into a category apart. There is nothing to rival with them in this respect. In neatness and precision they are superior, even, to the plates with which the works of the same Percier and Fontaine are illustrated. Henry Moses was, in fact, an original designer of remarkable merit and this work by him epitomizes the age of the Regency. It contains plates and culs-de-lampe, of only a few square inches in size, representing rooms filled with people, every detail of dress, furniture and ornament being in absolute harmony and accord. They form, in fact, the multum in parvo of the Conversation Piece. The delicacy of their stipple is unrivalled in the original. It is probable, indeed, that these are the finest and neatest engravings that have ever made their appearance between the covers of a book.

This forgotten artist, who survived until as late a period as the Franco-Prussian War, carries the history of the Conversation Piece into the scope of living memory. Long before he was dead the age of the photograph had arrived. The pioneers of that invention, as could be paralleled in the art of printing, have never been surpassed in their early efforts. A photograph by Octavius Hill, reproduced here (10), is an instance of what the Conversation Piece can achieve in this direction. These photographs, taken between seventy and eighty years ago, have never been improved upon and possess definite value as works of art. Another contemporary pioneer, Mr. Fox-Talbot, who worked at his Wiltshire home, Lacock Abbey, was no less successful (11). Octavius Hill and Fox-Talbot are to be classed, definitely, as artists. Close study of the primitives of the art of photography, of such men as Octavius Hill and Nadar, must improve the results to be obtained by the latest and most modern inventions of the camera maker.

Perhaps the intimacy of the informal photograph is to be compared with the purposes of the Conversation Piece. The graces of Van Dyck or Lely could not be imputed to that larger public which employed Zoffany and the innumerable lesser men to be mentioned in the body of this book. Their wish was to be represented at their natural ease surrounded by the objects or environment that they knew. The methods of the Dutch school, which were more popular with Englishmen than the magniloquence or the painted religion of the Italians, were quickly adapted to these new purposes. The grammar, so to speak, of Hogarth, of Zoffany, or of Copley, is Dutch in its origins and derivation. But the idiom and the inflections became English in the space of a generation. It would be impossible to mistake the nationality of the three painters who have been mentioned.

If we consider, now, the Conversation Piece as seen through the eyes

7

of its owners we have to admit that their security lay in the precision of its detail. It was in the exact resemblance of painted mantelpiece, or object of silver or of porcelain, that value and merit received their guarantee. The accessories of Zoffany were as valuable as his heads or clothes. This is a criterion by which it is, now, impermissible to judge a painting. Verisimilitude is no longer sought for in a picture, and is despised when found. But perhaps the consistent production of good minor paintings is only possible when this bait is allowed from the painter to the public. And it is likely, at least, to be paralleled by some improvement in the minor details and accessories of life.

Of these, there is the vindication in nearly every Conversation Piece that can be found. The details and appurtenances of the typical Georgian house are blended into harmony with the personalities of that age. But their importance to the future must depend upon what the future will bring. Never again, it is probable, will the cultured leisure of these figurants in silk and velvet find its repetition in our world that has begun to swarm. There is no room for leisure; no time for fine clothes. Then, the ticking of the clock was all the change in time. The same rules of taste governed a painting, a sonata, or the façade of a building. These rules were made for lesser men; but the great men worked outside them. Such laws were the safe grammar of competence; and until their importance is recognized, once more, the disharmony must continue.

The body of sound and second rate work depends for its creation upon the existence of formula and convention. This does not admit of contradiction, and ten minutes' drive in a motor car should convince anyone of its truth. Even the most beautiful of our towns and villages are disfigured by the constant evidence that this is so. Thatched cottages, or Georgian houses of red brick, show side by side with the worst examples of the cheap commercial builder. These stand in shameful proximity to the primitives of their art. In just this manner is the Conversation Piece the primitive of English painting, coming before water colour or landscape as the typical expression of the English genius. Its creation was due to Hogarth, the first great painter of our race. Gainsborough essayed it in his youth; and, after him, Zoffany and all the lesser men. We begin, therefore, with Hogarth. For it was in his hands that the Conversation Piece received its shape and foreshadowed its own future.

10. From a Photograph by Octavius Hill, taken in Edinburgh during the early 'Forties

11. From a Photograph by Fox-Talbot, probably taken at Lacock Abbey, *circa* 1842

12. THE WEDDING OF MR. STEPHEN BECKINGHAM AND MISS MARY COX

William Hogarth

CHAPTER II

WILLIAM HOGARTH

THE CONVERSATION PIECE owes its character and conception to the genius of Hogarth. He is the master of the school; the one or two exquisite Gainsboroughs, the tireless Devis, the ubiquitous Zoffany are but his pupils. Nearly unknown painters may contribute some of the most delightful pictures of the whole group, but it is always to Hogarth that our admiration returns. He invented the genre, formulated the principles and left unsurpassed examples. And the true stature of this artist is revealed when we consider that such interior scenes represent only a fraction of his output. The Conversation Piece was the whole life of Zoffany, but it was only a fragment of the talents of Hogarth.

Even so, the lesson of realism through informality is to be found in nearly everything that Hogarth painted. It was an essential point in his hatred of nonsense and fussiness. A contempt for idle pretence was the strength of Hogarth; but, in another sense, his ignorance was his weakness. The pride of his plain, blunt qualities convinced him of his own superior worth. He denied anything that he did not understand. Italian painting was mere foolishness; French art was but fashion and no permanence. He was convinced of his own merit. This was his genius and his shortcoming.

Lely and Kneller were no Englishmen. Hogarth would paint the first good portraits; attempt the grand style and excel in parable and comedy. His Sigismonda would outshine Correggio; in the Pool of Bethesda he would rival with Murillo. But Sigismonda and Bethesda failed. The picture was ridiculous and the fresco false and thin. That staircase at St. Bartholomew's Hospital was a project to which Hogarth should never have set his hand. Even the help of George Lambert, a skilful landscapist and scene painter, could not avail him. The genius of Hogarth was for drama; it was for satire, comedy or play. His portraits, Lord Lovat or Captain Coram, come under this heading. The Rake's Progress and the Harlot's Progress do the same. Marriage à la Mode, as was said by Horace Walpole, is a comedy by Molière. Beer Street and Gin Lane are ferocious satires. They are burlesques of the slums.

But, having refreshed our memories with his achievements, we narrow

9

the perspective and go back to his origins. It is important to do so, because the germ of the Conversation Piece of Hogarth is to be found in the earliest moments of his career. He was born, it will be remembered, in the parish of St. Bartholomew, in 1697; and before 1720 was bound apprentice to Mr. Ellis Gamble, the silversmith, of Cranbourn Street, Leicester Fields. His first work consisted in engraving coats of arms and heraldic devices upon pieces of silver. Several of these engravings by him have been identified with tolerable certainty. After a year or two at this employment he undertook prints for the booksellers, his best-known work in this direction being the twelve large plates that he designed for Hudibras, in 1726. Neither in this, nor in his other cuts, does his talent emerge to particular advantage. But, in the same year, Hogarth designed and engraved various shop bills and, in these, it can be said that his particular genius comes first to light. The shop bill that he made for his sister is a particularly happy specimen of his skill (6). It is a Conversation Piece in miniature. There are one or two more shop bills hardly less delightful; and out of his rather mysterious and unknown youth it is, perhaps, permissible to wonder if the hand of Hogarth had any concern in the splendid and robust engravings upon a certain punch bowl exhibited, in 1935, among the Huguenot silver at the Gallery of Messrs. Crichton. For these rollicking figures, smoking their long clay pipes, heavily bewigged and lurching genially as they straddle through the smoke, would seem to be the work of Hogarth and none other.

In his little shop bills there is already apparent the direction in which Hogarth was to excel. But, at this point, it is necessary to define the boundaries within which we can allow ourselves the freedom of this discussion. The Rake's Progress and Marriage à la Mode are, in a sense, Conversation Pieces, but their satirical or didactic purpose puts them outside our limits. The Conversation Piece must be pure play, and not comedy, nor satire. If it were otherwise, in the end it would be necessary to include George Cruikshank, and every illustrator such as Leech or 'Phiz,' until the subject would attain to impossible dimensions and become diverted from its true ideal, which is portraiture in natural and intimate surroundings. For the same reason, too, the splendid theatrical subjects by Zoffany, and the similar pictures of de Wilde, must be debarred. They form a school of painting, in themselves; and, for our subject, the Conversation Piece pure and simple is already sufficiently alarming in its extent.

If we develop our theme, working within those narrowed limits, the little shop bills of Hogarth's youth are seen to contain the prophecy of all that we will have to examine. They are the nucleus, or multum in parvo,

13. SCENE FROM "THE INDIAN EMPEROR"

William Hogarth

Mary, Countess of Ilchester

14. THE WESTERN FAMILY

William Hogarth   *National Gallery of Ireland, Dublin*

15. THE GRAHAM CHILDREN

William Hogarth   *National Gallery, London*

of his art. From this whole we must subtract what is of importance to ourselves. The anti-Gallic Hogarth is evident from the first. His solid and more Handelian pencil designed the sensible and not excessive rococo of these scrolls. Hogarth was the middle class Englishman, without a trace of the Celt in him, a typical inhabitant of the plain and manly houses of the metropolis. Hogarth is the truth of appearances; and, in the whole of his century, he is almost alone in this. Who, but Hogarth, would have painted the horrors of Beer Street and Gin Lane? As well as being anti-Gallic, Hogarth is the anti-rococo, or anti-Arcadian of his time. Like other men of his class he hated poverty and hated riches.

His instincts, which denied him the French or Italian taste, had more in keeping with the Dutch School of painters. It is known that Hogarth never visited the Low Countries; but pictures of Terburg and de Hoogh must have come under his notice in London. Those masters of the interior scene, together with Metsu, with Dou, and with many lesser men, were his predecessors in the Conversation Piece. Pieter de Hoogh, the great master of this style, was possessed of a patient technique to which Hogarth with his robust vigour could not aspire. But the pictures of de Hoogh had been painted fifty years earlier: they belong to the generation of 1650 to 1680. And their purpose and aim were entirely different from the motives which inspired Hogarth. The pleasure of de Hoogh lay in the play of light; in its dissemination into the interior stillness of a room. He liked to catch its contact upon marble and on china; its effects on silk or velvet were his toys of skill. The paint was worked by him until it took on the actual counterfeit of fur or silver, the grain of new wood or the lights in copper. Perpetual stillness holds his pictures. They are a moment in a summer afternoon; and, could you listen, you would hear the leaves brush against the windows and the bee, heavy laden, bump upon the mullion. They are the light of day but not the living blood. They are not characterized or dramatized. De Hoogh in this respect stands to Hogarth as Richardson or Fanny Burney to Dickens or Balzac. It was the gift of Hogarth to paint character and drama into the scene. This was his interest; and, while his competence expressed itself in detail, the accessories are props or units of the play.

The contemporary painter with whom it is most easy to compare Hogarth is the Dutchman, Cornelius von Troost (1697-1750). This little known artist, who is scarcely represented in our National Gallery, can best be seen at The Hague, where there is a small room of his pictures in the Mauritshuis. It is certain that Troost knew the work of Hogarth, through his prints; but Hogarth, more probably, lived in ignorance of his rival.

Troost is, in fact, a good standard by which to judge the rank of Hogarth. He painted many interior scenes, and subjects taken from comedies, mostly in gouache, in which medium he is without a rival. His gouaches have a clear opaque light, reminiscent of Liotard, and he delights, it might be said, in white walls, blue china and black clothes. Troost presents to us the burgher life of Amsterdam, the personages of those brick houses giving on to the linden shaded waters, and the curious burlesques or comedies of that city of canals. These are rendered with a touch of Callot; and they are in the scale of Callot, or of Liotard. This is the true stature of Troost. There is a delight to be gained from the fresh colours of his gouache such as the heavy pigment of Hogarth cannot give; but the Englishman is a master and the Dutchman a petit maître.

The importance of Hogarth is in the thoroughness of his achievement. A picture by his hand is carried down to the smallest detail in anecdotal dramatization, as in the progress of a plot. No point is forced or hurried. His accessories are left to be discovered and do not obtrude. Thus a picture by Hogarth gains invariably upon improved acquaintance. It proves its haphazard points, like a good play seen a second time. His paintings must be taken at the speed they set. That is slowly methodical, for Hogarth has the weight and solidity of Handel. There is the same assurance of sound workmanship. But no analogy in music fits close to Hogarth. His is the literary talent of the Englishman, first seen in painting. He is Congreve or Dickens taken to the brush. The same talent was at work in Hogarth which has given us Kipps, and, if we dare say so, Little Tich or Nellie Wallace. It is one phase of the English or Cockney genius. In the case of Hogarth it can be said that he conforms strictly to the tenets of his kind and that he is true to its principles in every instance and in all respects.

Those pictures by his hand with which we are here concerned form no inconsiderable a part of his output. It is usual to date his fame from the completion of the Harlot's Progress, in 1733. Three years before this he had married the daughter of Sir James Thornhill, the only considerable English fresco painter and a person of unrecognized eminence in the international, or Italianate world of the baroque. By 1730, therefore, Hogarth was in receipt of enough income to marry, and it is important, in this connection, that two at least of his most important Conversation Pieces should date from these very years. The scene from 'The Indian Emperor' was painted in 1731, and the group of the Cholmondeley family in 1732. These are pictures, in each case, of important people in the world of fashion. Careful and accurate drawings must have been taken for them, and they

William Hogarth

16.   THE CHOLMONDELEY FAMILY

The Marquess of Cholmondeley

17.   A FAMILY PARTY

William Hogarth   *Sir Herbert Cook, Bart.*

18.   "TASTE IN HIGH LIFE"

William Hogarth   *The Earl of Iveagh*

19. THE BROTHERS CLARKE, OF SWAKELEYS

William Hogarth

By courtesy of the Tooth Galleries

20. A FAMILY GROUP

William Hogarth

National Gallery, London

21. THE PRICE FAMILY

William Hogarth

represent an effort at composition on his part which is at least as important as the long preparations for the Harlot's Progress, or Marriage à la Mode. Hogarth was thirty-four years old when he painted 'The Indian Emperor.' He spared no pains over the picture which, in the result, is one of the most striking things in the whole of English art. It would be true, indeed, to say that this is the first important composition by an English painter.

This picture (13), which has hung for a century and more at Holland House, has for subject a performance, by children, of Dryden's play, 'The Indian Emperor; or The Conquest of Mexico.' The scene is taking place inside a large room, one end of which has been curtained off in order to form a stage. It is at the house of Mr. Conduit, Master of the Mint. The diagonal action of the picture, as the plate will show, has allowed of a double set of portraits. The four little children who are acting form, in themselves, a masterpiece of painting. In the audience are the Duke of Cumberland, Princess Mary, Princess Louisa, the Duke and Duchess of Richmond, the Duke of Montagu, the Earl of Pomfret, Captain Poyntz, and others. The grouping of so many figures is natural and quite unstilted; while two little girls in the front row of the audience are as inimitable as those upon the stage. Their dress, too, is amusingly contrasted, for the child actors are in regular stage clothes; little Cortez in slashed doublet and the three little girls with plumed headdresses. The room is a fine and recent interior, of George I or II, with a splendid fireplace, fine cornices and a good group of sculpture in the corner near the stage. There is an exciting and unexpected quality about the whole composition. The slant play of the characters gives it novelty and never, perhaps, has a plot in portraiture been more skilfully conceived. No one in the French or Italian painting of the day could have contrived that solidity. Goya, a later painter who might have seized upon a like excuse, lacked the patience to render the background, or would have hurried the pace and been sardonic with the audience. The scene from 'The Indian Emperor' is, therefore, the chef d'œuvre of the Conversation Piece.

The painting of the Graham children, now in the National Gallery (15), shows Hogarth in another mood. The focus is much nearer. It is a delightful picture; but so readily to be seen by the public that it hardly requires description. So we turn to the Cholmondeley family, of 1732 (16). This again, in the language of the old dictionaries of painting, is one of Hogarth's capital performances. The Conversation Piece of the future, in the hands of Zoffany or Copley, was much influenced by its manner and detail. Hogarth, once again, has achieved a double composition, a design, as it were, in two compartments, by placing the figures in

13

a library which is divided from a picture gallery by a booklined partition. The family sit, formally, in the library and two little boys play, informally, in the gallery. They have just caught their feet in a corner of the carpet, which makes a foil to the dignity of their parents; and, in compensation, as if to placate the father and mother for the fidgeting and interruption, Hogarth has painted a pair of cupids above their heads playing with a tassel cord and pulling back a curtain. It is almost the only time that Hogarth tolerated the ridiculous and the unreal, for so it must have seemed to his matter of fact mind. Also, about the figure of Lord Cholmondeley, himself, there is the trace of the French influence, a touch of Largillière. This picture, therefore, must be related to a time when Hogarth, as was his wont, had set himself out in deliberate competition with his foreign rivals. Such portrait groups as that by Largillière, of Louis XIV and the Grand Dauphin, now in the Wallace Collection, must have been in the mind of Hogarth when he painted this group of Lord Cholmondeley and his family. And, once again, Hogarth triumphs in the solidity and character imputed to his sitters. Largillière was no psychologist. In comparison with Hogarth he was a flatterer and a lover of fine surfaces.

Another portrait group by Hogarth which is no less delightful is the Wedding of Mr. Stephen Beckingham (12). This is one of the most attractive of minor pictures. It has not the importance of the scene from the 'Indian Emperor,' and yet no painting could be better in its way. Mr. Stephen Beckingham is marrying Miss Mary Cox of Kidderminster. They are standing at the altar steps. The clergyman is a glorious piece of characterization; and so is an old gentleman, perhaps he is Mr. Cox of Kidderminster, dressed in dark clothes and a fine white wig, who leans on his walking stick and listens attentively to the words of the marriage service. In the foreground there are two charming bridesmaids, one of them with her fan. A magnificent Turkey carpet cascades across the front of the picture. The background is a church interior of typical Queen Anne architecture with splendid coffered ceiling, Corinthian pilasters, curved cornices and attic windows to let in the light. A man and a boy look down from a gallery and two amorini empty a cornucopia above the head of the bride. The classical architecture is rendered with splendid fidelity. Good sense and solidity breathe out from the walls. There is a tradition that this interior is that of St. Benet's, Paul's Wharf; but Dr. G. C. Williamson says it is, without doubt, St. Martin's-in-the-Fields. This must be the most charming picture of a wedding ever painted. The figures fit with perfect ease into the architectural background. The clothes are new; the church not long finished; and even the tombs, or tablets upon the walls, are the entire product of

22. "THE BROKEN FAN"

William Hogarth

Lord Northbrook

23. PORTRAIT GROUP OF A FISHING PARTY

William Hogarth

The Dulwich Gallery

their time. Everything in sight in this picture has the ease and dignity of Handel.

It might be hoped that there would be many more portrait groups by Hogarth of this degree of merit. No painter of Conversation Pieces had this skill in the invention of a plot or drama. It is as though he would not undertake a subject until a sufficient excuse presented itself for the assembly of as many figures as were stipulated in the canvas. But, unfortunately, Hogarth had all his other activities to consider. A series such as Marriage à la Mode or the Rake's Progress achieved more sensation with the public. They were copied in engraving and the prints sold far and wide. Also, the didactic purpose in such pictures led Hogarth into the satirical field, where the Dunciad side of his genius found inimitable opportunity. He was too much of a dramatist to neglect this direction and it came to take up his energies to the exclusion of everything else. There are, for this reason, but few other groups by him, and none of them quite as important as those described. His reputation in that field was too early established, and henceforth he addressed himself to the larger public. This is the loss of art, because, as a moralist and a satirist, he ceased to be a painter.

Nevertheless he has left us other groups which come into our category, but they are invariably small in scale, and painted, we might think, in the intervals of other employment. This is to the lasting detriment of English art. It would not be too much to say that the subtraction of Hogarth from portrait painting, and the addition to it of Gainsborough, are two melancholy chapters in our history. Hogarth deserted drama for satire and farce; and Gainsborough left poetry behind for prose. But Hogarth was our first native painter. He had not the lyrical gift of Gainsborough, of which the portrait of Mr. and Mrs. Andrews (71) is the immortal expression. There is no picture of Hogarth which has that quality of youth. Hogarth, like Handel, will have aged young. He was heavy and solid, in full-bottomed wig. Compared to Hogarth, that picture of the young man and woman among the cornfields is like a work of the Salzburg period of Mozart. It is fresh and spontaneous, like the finest rococo, while Hogarth is more grave and serious. The degree of his finish is the Handelian termination. It is dignified and pompous, even in its humour. It is a tragic thought that Gainsborough was led from landscape into portraiture for want of money and that Hogarth left portrait painting for satire because it paid him better. These two men, who are the greatest figure painters that our country has produced, could have maintained that peculiarly English invention of the Conversation Piece at the level of their highest talents. But Gainsborough early deserted it, and Hogarth only touched at it now and again.

15

Hogarth, it cannot be stressed too often, was the first English painter; and, as is so often the case with the pioneer, subsequent effort has never surpassed the original. He never, it is true, painted his subjects successfully in a landscape setting. This was left for Gainsborough and Zoffany to do. His excellence, as we have said, was in plot and disposition. None of his subjects are painted in idleness and doing nothing. They are always actors in some unconscious play. Hogarth favoured the detail of incident and not of execution. He never attempts to make his drama anything but a picture. The laborious counterfeit of silk or silver, the play of objects in a shining mirror, the stitch by stitch of Gerard Dou, mere virtuosity in representation, had no appeal for him any more than had the brick by brick rendering of van der Heyden. The finish of the cabinet picture, its essential stillness, its meticulous silence, were an interruption of the action. It was the dialogue of character that interested this typical town dweller, who, indeed, like the true Cockney, might never have seen the green fields or waving trees of the country. He is the Londoner of iron railings and the area, whose shade we must look for, now, along Doughty Street or Bedford Square, in some remaining row or terrace of early Georgian London. It is rare, indeed, to find a single flower in Hogarth. His world was the brick London, expectant of November fog. He had no sense of antiquity or time. London was new built from the fire; and it was the world of his own day that he painted, of that generation who had seen the hundred new churches of Queen Anne raising their pepper castor steeples of white Portland stone into the metropolitan air. Hawksmoor or Gibbs were the architects of this transformation. It was Gibbs who built the church in which we can watch the marriage of Mr. Stephen Beckingham. The pair of splendid paintings by Canaletto, at Goodwood, are contemporary evidence of this new London. The flashing white steeples of the churches diminish down the distance, as the curve of the river runs down to distant Greenwich, and they are as conspicuous a feature of the view as the pagoda in any scene of celestial China. While they were painted, somewhere in London Hogarth was abroad in that world of brick and white stone. Canaletto gives the cold Palladian exterior; and Hogarth, the warmer London of within.

The deflection of this splendid painter into caricature and satire has made much of his mature work unpalatable and, to a later age, almost unintelligible. He raked Grub Street with his fire, but the names and identity of his victims are nearly unknown to us. This misdirection of his energies is paralleled in Alexander Pope. Both men had a potency of aggression which impelled them into attack. Pope had a weapon or sting which he was constrained to use. The Dunciad is an inferno of mud and

William Hogarth

24.   CONVERSATION GROUP

25. A FAMILY GROUP

Artist Unknown   *Lady Hudson*

26. AN ENGLISH PARTY

Artist Unknown   *National Gallery, London*

filth. Like the open sewers of the slums, the pestilence of its vapours poisons and overcomes the sprawling inhabitants. It is the truth beneath appearances. The vileness of the back streets is in contradiction to the fine façade, the grace and glitter of the century. Hogarth, also, had his venom, and was not content to be attacked without retaliation. He is, by reason of this, the only painter of his age by whom the unflattering truth is told. Beer Street and Gin Lane, the Four Stages of Cruelty, are his criticism of the age in which he lived. But the wilder sorts of fantasy obsessed his brain. He had not the intellect, the scholarship of Pope. His floating, unconnected frenzy passed, almost, to insanity. There is a touch of madness in his Analysis of Beauty. The humour has gone out of him and he has become serious. The crabbed, contorted images spell forth his contempt of both stupidity and learning. But hallucination, or deformity, has not improved him. It is not his genius which has led him to this; but a moral message, or a verbal meaning. These are not paintings, but caricatures or posters for the nightmares of a Dean Swift. Perhaps they are time wasted, when his other talents are considered. And yet, in his old age, the Shrimp Girl, and the group of heads of his servants, show the new and free development which was taking place in him. These are loosely painted and the handling is different from any picture that he had yet achieved. It is our misfortune that there is no more considerable work of his, dating from this time, in which pure painting has been his purpose and not satire.

But not one of his outstanding Conversation Pieces belongs to his last years; and those that remain to be described are small and, for the most part, unimportant. Quite a numerous group, however, could be assembled of very small pictures, belonging, it is almost certain, to the decade of 1730 to 1740. There must be many more of these in existence than is generally supposed, scattered up and down England in country houses. Taken together they would form an imposing group, but their interest dwindles, one by one. Many of them are restricted to only one or two figures and can, therefore, scarcely be called Conversation Pieces. An excellent but small painting, belonging to Sir Herbert Cook, at Richmond, is an exception to this (17). There are six figures in the composition and the action includes a tea party, a man playing with a dog, and a man and woman playing a game at a table, a splendid example of Hogarth's insistence upon excuse and reason in his poses. This painting might be described as a masculine Pietro Longhi.

Another good Conversation Piece by Hogarth is The Broken Fan (22), belonging to Lord Northbrook. The group consists of three women, who are said to be Lady Thornhill, Hogarth's mother-in-law; her daughter, who became the painter's wife; and Hogarth's own sister. Lady Thornhill is dressed in widow's weeds, which must date the picture from some year subsequent to 1734. The plot of the piece has for its action the playing of two little spaniels, one of whom is running away with a broken fan held in its mouth. The furniture in the room is elaborate and Venetian in style and the artist's sister is reading at a table covered with a Turkey rug. Hogarth's device of the double composition is made use of again, for the table at which she is sitting is in an archway giving on to another room behind. He has achieved a most intense and lifelike portrait of the two younger women; and the whole picture is an admirable specimen of his powers and an ostensible and typical Hogarth. No one but he could have achieved its rich and solid impasto. The Lady's Last Stake, belonging to the Duke of Richmond, is a much larger canvas, and is supposed to be the portrait of Mrs. Thrale or Mrs. Piozzi. It is, also, known as Virtue in Danger. Mrs. Thrale, in old age, seems to have regarded her appearance on this canvas as a youthful indiscretion and gave at least two different versions of why she was thus painted. The composition, by some curious chance, is much more like a Copley than a Hogarth. It has, indeed, a quite extraordinary resemblance to the Sitwell family by that painter, which will be noticed at a later part of this book (98).

In the Dulwich Gallery there is to be found a delightful little fishing picture by Hogarth, treated in a manner that is a curious prophecy of Gainsborough (23). There are, also, to be seen in the National collections a fine group of people breakfasting or having tea, in the National Gallery (20), and the painting of the Western family in the Dublin Gallery (14). A splendid drawing of a family group, from the British Museum, is reproduced in order to show the bold, free grouping of Hogarth and the manner in which the disposition of his ten figures into their groups or clusters was established by him before he proceeded to portraiture proper (24). A painting of the brothers Clarke, of Swakeleys, who are drinking wine round a table (19), has deep and significant resemblance to the engraving upon the silver punch bowl aforementioned; while it is of interest to compare it as well with a somewhat similar group illustrated later in the book also by that forgotten painter Gawen Hamilton (82). The attribution in the title of Fig. 19 to Hogarth should be corrected to Hamilton. Not the least amusing part of this quaint picture is the identical likeness in all six brothers. And one of them, who would seem to be the eldest, if, indeed, they are all brothers and not cousins, is sitting in a gilt and mahogany chair that should be the delight of the connoisseur in fine furniture.

There remain to be described two little paintings, both dating from a

27. LORD GEORGE GRAHAM IN HIS CABIN

William Hogarth

National Maritime Museum, Greenwich

28.   QUEEN CHARLOTTE AND HER TWO ELDEST CHILDREN

John Zoffany

Reproduced by gracious permission of H.M. The King

late period in Hogarth's life, and both presenting exceptional features which put them into a different category from any of his pictures so far noticed. Taste in High Life (18) is the first of these. It belongs, strictly speaking, to that category of his paintings which is satirical in intention and should not, therefore, come under discussion as a Conversation Piece, but its inclusion is irresistible, on more than one count. The story behind this picture is that it was commissioned by an old lady, Miss Edwardes, who was imbued with a hatred of the French nation. This project was entered upon with alacrity by Hogarth, who was a confirmed Xenophobe. He has made the picture into a satire upon the French and Italian fashions of 1742.

The action consists, so to speak, in the mincing manner of the principal actors. An old lady and gentleman, attired in the height of fashion, are talking together in an ecstasy of affectation over a tiny porcelain cup and saucer. The old lady wears a dress, covered with a pattern of full-blown roses, which is distended by an enormous hoop. Her shape is a perfect pyramid with a rounded base. The old gentleman, in contrast, is thin and natty. He carries one of the muffs which make their appearance, also, in the fashionable interiors, or parlatorios, of Guardi. His hair is tied with a black silk bow and he wears an immensely long plaited pigtail. He is a mass of affectation, and so feeble that he can scarcely stand. On the floor in front of this curious pair a monkey, elaborately dressed and wearing a laced cocked hat, is reading a paper with the aid of a spyglass. The subsidiary action in the background is supplied by a very handsome young woman, said to be the Kitty Fisher who was afterwards painted by Reynolds, who is wasting her time by her attentions to a little turbaned negro page. He is sitting on the corner of a table, holding in his hands a china figure of a mandarin. The walls of the room are hung with portraits of Italian ballet dancers and satirical pictures, conceived of by Hogarth, but difficult to follow without a key to their meaning, because, by a lapse in his dramatic convention, Hogarth painted them against, and not on behalf of, the actors in his drama. They have, that is to say, no rightful appearance upon the walls of this room, in which no satire upon fashion would ever have been permitted. This little blunder apart, Taste in High Life is most certainly a marvel of satire and, as a picture, occupies an important place in Hogarth's work. Its contemporary truth is so biting and to the point that its application has become timeless and could be made as appropriate to the year in which we are living.

The other picture (27) is very different in character. Not only this, but it is strange and novel in scene. Indeed, no other picture of the kind has been attempted by a good painter. It is the interior of a cabin, on board ship. Lord George Graham, the son of the Duke of Montrose, and, at the time, a Captain in the Navy, is seen eating a somewhat perfunctory breakfast. Instead, he is smoking a very long pipe and listening to music. He is dressed in mufti, even, indeed, in high fashion, which dates the picture, for uniform was only introduced in the Navy in 1748. The music comes from a black boy who beats a drum, while a short, stout, middle-aged man sings a ballad from a sheet that he holds in his hand. Another, younger man, for whom a place has been laid at the table, listens attentively with a book in his hands. In the background a cabin boy, in white cap and apron, brings in a roasted chicken on a silver dish. Such is the picture; but it is given a distinction of its own by the delightful ease and informality of the captain and by the slant and peculiar wooden architecture of the ship. Nothing is at the accustomed angle. The windows of the cabin slope outwards from the floor up; the boards of the ceiling appear to run in different directions all at once; and the wall is panelled and ornamented with Corinthian pilasters, delightfully gilt, but starting at an angle by the windows and gradually righting themselves into perpendicular as they pass out of sight, out of the canvas. The scene, in fact, is as unfamiliar in painting as the interior of an aeroplane. This imparts to it a peculiar and almost unfair advantage over the ordinary Conversation Piece. There is no more delightful picture by Hogarth than this. We may imagine that it is a sea ballad that is being sung. The topgallants of other ships of the fleet can be seen through the windows. It is, therefore, right and appropriate that this little picture should now rest in the National Maritime Museum at Greenwich, in that fine palace of Portland stone which contains the painted hall by Sir James Thornhill, close to Nelson's pigtail, and among the portraits and relics of the Navy which must make this a sacred spot to Englishmen.

The description of this picture must close our remarks upon the Conversation Pieces of Hogarth. The scene from 'The Indian Emperor,' the Wedding of Mr. Stephen Beckingham, and this cabin interior are sufficient, in themselves, to illustrate his talent. Hogarth is our first painter and, apart from Gainsborough, the greatest of our figure painters. He can stand comparison with any artist, of any country, in his century. He was the typical Englishman but, in order to assess his talent, it is necessary to compare him with de Hoogh or Metsu, with Terburg or Jan Steen. He emerges out of this comparison with more vitality than they possessed and a less patient technique. But there is not one of them who could have composed the scene from 'The Indian Emperor.' It is, in fact, among his

Conversation Pieces that much of Hogarth's talent is dispersed. Nor is it at all certain that some of the finest of these pictures may not still be hidden and unknown. The discovery of a new Conversation Piece by Hogarth must always remain one of the most delightful possibilities in English art. For, with Hogarth, scale is not everything and often it is his smallest pictures that are the best.

CHAPTER III

JOHN ZOFFANY

IT was a saying of Talleyrand that no one had tasted the pleasures of life who had not lived before the French Revolution. That ancient and cynical mask was speaking, of course, more particularly of his own country, but his remark has an equal application to England. It is to be understood, since it was Talleyrand who said it, that he refers only to the affluent or well to do. The poor were no part of the visual world to him. For all that mattered to Talleyrand they did not exist. It is the same with the Conversation Piece. This class of picture was only concerned with those who led their lives freely in surroundings of luxury and ease. And it may be remarked that, where England is concerned, the Conversation Piece which is the mirror of our social history of that time has been, also, in some sense, its guarantee. For the great majority of these pictures still belong to the descendants of their original owners. In many houses they even hang in the same dining room in which they were first placed. They have occupied, in fact, a privileged position from which the changes of time have not dislodged them. They are evidence of the past while they look down upon and are witness of the present.

Of all this testimony to an age that was finer to the eyes there is no delineator more faithful in detail than Zoffany. He is, in every essential, the ideal painter of the Conversation Piece. His name must stand for that, as much as the painted ceiling must stand for Tiepolo. The mention of him has immediate association with that kind of painting in which he is unrivalled master. In question of stature there can be no comparison between Tiepolo and Zoffany, but, at least, a rare competence is implicit in his name and he is not remote from us like that last of the old masters. Zoffany is a minor painter, let us admit that, but it is only of very recent years that the consistent level of his paintings has been realized. Nor can our contemporary age, whose painters have lost the power of grouping figures and are afraid to paint things as they are, afford to be contemptuous towards an artist of his solid achievement. We may have the sensibility to see that he was a painter not of the first order; while we possess, in our own age, no living painter of his competence and technique.

22

Zoffany, like Lely and like Kneller, was a foreigner. His father was a Bohemian Jew who worked as a cabinetmaker at Prague and, later, in Germany. It was there that Johann Zoffany was born, at Frankfort-on-Main, in 1733. He developed talent at a very early age and was placed by his father in the studio of a certain Michael Speer, who had studied at Naples under Solimena. In 1750 Zoffany travelled in Italy as far as Rome; but his career really begins with his arrival in London, in about 1760. For a time he was near to starvation and only earned small sums by painting clock dials for Stephen Rimbault, the famous clockmaker. Three or four of these are still in existence and are reproduced by Dr. G. C. Williamson. Soon after this time he entered the studio of Benjamin Wilson, made the acquaintance of Garrick who was to remain his lifelong friend, and by dint of hard work improved his circumstances until he is to be found, in 1765, living in Lincoln's Inn Fields and already celebrated as a painter of portrait groups.

It is to be remarked that the Jewish ancestry of Zoffany is an important factor in his art. He is, indeed, the first Jewish painter of any eminence and, probably, the greatest whom that gifted race has yet produced. Their talent is for assimilation and Zoffany is no inconspicuous instance of this. Coming into England as an alien, he was able to seize upon and develop certain characteristics in nationality, as the result of which his paintings are typical, almost to a theatrical degree, of the English scene. At the same time, underlying this, there is his Southern German origin. He came to us, it must be remembered, out of rococo Germany. Zoffany must have seen the churches, for instance, of the brothers Asam and such frescoes as those that decorate the vaults and cupolas of Zwiefalten and Ottobeuren. This school of painters, Troger, Altomonte, Daniel Gran, which derived from Padre Pozzo and from Tiepolo, was at work in every great monastery of Bavaria and Austria during his youth, and on his journey to Italy he could not fail to have seen many paintings of the kind. There are, also, the evidences in his own work, to those who know the Neapolitan school, that Zoffany had studied under a pupil of Solimena. His clear colour came out of these antecedents, and the flowing and ready ease of his composition.

On coming to England, Zoffany applied himself to the study of Hogarth. That great painter died in 1764, the year before Zoffany was established with some comfort in Lincoln's Inn Fields. Nor was the study of Hogarth a difficult undertaking, for engravings of most of his pictures were readily obtainable. The rest of his schooling was in the Dutch painters, the masters of still life no less than Mieris or Metsu. His Italian journey had given Zoffany an experience which was lacking to Hogarth, who never left

23

England except to go to Calais. His ease and quickness came from that; while from the Dutch painters he learned to render the accessories in a perfection of finish which was quite foreign to Hogarth's manly humour. This photographic accuracy had a sure attraction for his patrons and he was to embark, as we shall see, upon several paintings in which the display of his virtuosity was the only object. He was less masculine than Hogarth: and his results came from meticulous carefulness rather than from inspiration. Hogarth carried things by his personality: Zoffany by his execution. But Zoffany had, also, another advantage over Hogarth. This consisted in his ability to paint landscape. He was able, in fact, to take the Conversation Piece out of doors. Zoffany was, therefore, better equipped at nearly every point than Hogarth. But Hogarth had genius: and Zoffany, only competence and talent. Nevertheless, since the whole of his long life was devoted to painting Conversation Pieces almost to the exclusion of anything else, Zoffany by his painstaking care has left a large number of delightful pictures.

If it is characteristic of the Jews to assimilate the nationality of those among whom they go to live, then Zoffany is as true to this virtue of his race as Offenbach, or Meyerbeer, or Johann Strauss. Offenbach, a Jew from Cologne, is typical to us, as he was to his contemporaries, of the Paris of Napoleon III; Meyerbeer was, by turns, Italian, Prussian, or Parisian; while Johann Strauss, who was partly of Spanish Jewish origin, is the picture of Vienna. No less is Zoffany the delineator of one side of the English life of his time. And this is given us, without exaggeration, and in candour. His Conversation Pieces are the interiors of Adam or Wyatt. The latter half of the eighteenth century in its elegance lives for us and is to be seen counterfeited on his canvases. He would paint his sitters among their most treasured possessions, gathered round them as if for tomb burial in the pyramid or mound. Certain of his pictures are, for this reason, the perfect illustration of their epoch.

The hard clearness of his lens has been helped by other considerations. Zoffany was a confirmed addict of the theatre, to the extent that a great section of his work consisted in theatrical portraiture. He was as fond of the play as Hogarth. This was his school of grouping and of action. The necessary quickness in the seizing of an attitude must have been of great help to him when planning out the composition of some large group or family. His German love for detail then asserted itself over the minutiae of the action so that the accessories are rendered with exaggerated clearness, as in a shaft of sunlight, or from the light off snow outside the windows. In his best groups, the Dutton family (29) or the Willoughby de Broke picture (44), there is something unmistakably German in the finish. And

24

John Zoffany

29. THE DUTTON FAMILY

Daniel H. Farr, Esq.

John Zoffany

The Duke of Atholl

30. JOHN, THIRD DUKE OF ATHOLL, AND HIS FAMILY

yet the effect of the whole is so characteristic of England that, by no possibility, could any other land or its inhabitants be depicted. Zoffany was one of the truest theatrical painters that has ever lived, and his dramatic sense was alive to the smallest detail. He was the ideal audience; not, like Hogarth, the actor in the play.

By 1765, therefore, with Hogarth dead and no one to take his place, we find Zoffany set up in London. He was to remain here, with two notable intervals, until his death in 1810. For forty years he was incessantly at work. His two absences were from 1773 till 1779, when he lived in Florence and in Vienna ; and from 1783 till 1790, during which time he was away in India. But even the subtraction of thirteen years from the total of his residence in London leaves him with nearly thirty years of achievement. And his huge output of paintings more than accounts for that passage of time. When the pictures that he painted in Florence and in India are added to this we are confronted with so much work, of nearly even merit, that it is difficult to determine which are his best paintings. It would seem, though, since his theatrical subjects do not concern us here, that his Conversation Pieces can be grouped into three main divisions. There are his feats of virtuosity, such pictures as the Tribuna (33), the Towneley marbles (37) and the group of the Sharp family (32), things which are more dazzling as technique than successful as works of art; there are the groups of nabobs whom he painted in India; and, thirdly, there is the ordinary Conversation Piece, a very numerous group of his pictures in which, perhaps, the Dutton family and the Willoughby de Broke picture are his finest achievement. But it is invidious to say this; for the moment the words are written we remember the picture of Queen Charlotte in an interior of Buckingham Palace (28), the Minuet in the Glasgow Gallery (50), the Drummond family (45), or the two pictures of Mr. and Mrs. Garrick (38, 39). To make a categorical statement, where Zoffany's Conversation Pieces are concerned, would be as senseless as to declare which are the best of Haydn's string quartets. It is only permissible to speak of what one has seen; and, in the case of Zoffany, as of Haydn, the known is but a portion of the unknown. It is true, at least, that these three divisions of his work can be established; and, since Zoffany was a painter in whom it is unnecessary to look for progress, since his achievement remained at the same level throughout his life, it is the simple course to keep within these categories and not to pursue him through a maze of dates. But this resolution we temper to our convenience in order to preserve the liberty of the reader.

One of the earliest of his Conversation Pieces, dating from 1765, is the group of John, 3rd Duke of Atholl, and his family (30). It was painted in the year in which that nobleman resigned the sovereignty of the Isle of Man into the hands of George III. According to Dr. G. C. Williamson, the landscape background to this picture, a delightful river scene complete with a swan and a weeping willow, is the work of another painter, Charles Stewart, who was engaged at Blair Castle painting the scenery of Tayside in a series of five landscapes for the dining room. Dr. Williamson reproduces the receipt of Zoffany for this picture, from which it is proved that the painter received twenty guineas for each of the nine portraits upon the canvas.

In 1770 Zoffany first exhibited in the Royal Academy, and from that year his most notable successes were to be seen upon the walls of Burlington House. Two years after this, the Life School in the Royal Academy made its appearance, now the property of H.M. the King. It was a picture that aroused much excited comment at the time, but it is a secondary performance on the part of Zoffany in comparison with the paintings that he was soon to produce.

In the same year there appeared 'The Lapidaries,' a portrait of Peter Dollond, the optician, with his assistant. This was a commission from George III and still hangs at Windsor Castle. It can be described as a small virtuoso piece, for it gave Zoffany an opportunity to lavish his skill upon the smallest details of glass and steel. Dollond, an old man with spectacles pushed up on to his turban, stands only a yard or two away from the spectator, and in the direct light of a window in front of which he is sitting. All the instruments of his craft of spectacle maker are round him, or upon the shelves high above his head, and each single object asserts its individuality in the morning light. It is a tour de force, or deliberate sample of Zoffany's powers, not a picture. And yet, partly owing to the geniality of the old man portrayed in it, we may wish that it had been possible chronologically, or otherwise, to have the portrait by Zoffany of Thomas Tompion the clock-maker, or of Paul Lamerie posed with his crucible and in the midst of his silver. Alas! that this picture cannot be called a Conversation Piece, and so is not among the illustrations to this book.

This little canvas provokes an obvious comparison with Wright of Derby, in his picture The Orreries, painted in 1766, but the allusion is at once dispelled if we contrast it, here, with another small picture that Zoffany was to paint a year or two later, in 1773, for the Infante Ferdinando of Parma. This comes, in a sense, into the same category of his work as 'The Lapidaries,' for it is a study of figures, in small, but as near as possible to the focus of the eyes, and possessed, therefore, of an unreal realism and vitality. The subject is some wandering musicians and the picture admini-

John Zoffany   31.   THE COWPER AND GORE FAMILIES

Lady Desborough

John Zoffany   32.   A MUSICAL PARTY ON THE THAMES

Miss Olive Lloyd-Baker

33.   THE TRIBUNA   *Reproduced by gracious permission of H.M. The King*

John Zoffany

sters a slight shock to the senses, hanging, as it still does, in the Gallery at Parma, close to Correggio and to Cima da Conegliano. Also, this little picture is an instructive commentary upon Zoffany's nationality, for in spite of his study of Hogarth while in England, there is here no possible link or connection with Hogarth. Zoffany becomes German again, in this instance, or the name of Liotard comes into the mind, but it is a Liotard in violent motion, enough for the figures to shake the pastel or gouache from their clothes. The cosmopolitan nationality of Zoffany is asserting itself in this curious little picture.

But we return, now, to what may be the most delightful picture ever painted by Zoffany. This is the group of Queen Charlotte and her two elder children in an interior of Old Buckingham House (28). It now hangs in the great corridor at Windsor, near to its companion piece of the Queen, her sister and her two brothers. Windsor Park is the background to that charming scene and it is almost superfluous, where Queen Charlotte is concerned, to say that a few of her numerous family of children are grouped round her. But that picture must yield in every way to its sister piece, which is certainly one of the master works of Zoffany.

Queen Charlotte, who is dressed in white satin, is sitting at her dressing table. It is a court dress, with elaborately panniered skirt and a richly worked corsage. She wears a ruched bow or ribbon round her neck. The Prince of Wales and the Duke of York, two little children of three or four years old, are standing by her knee; but the Prince of Wales is dressed in Roman or heroic uniform, with crested helm and carrying a spear, and the Duke of York is a little turbaned Oriental. The Queen is thinking or listening, while she strokes the head of a big mastiff who is a good deal larger than either of the children. Perhaps she hears the roar of the traffic through the open window. It is the horses of the Piccadilly coaches. The dressing table and mirror, which have muslin flounces down to the ground, are painted with a delightful and cool airiness, the transparency of their pattern making a contrast to the Turkey carpet upon the floor. But, even more, it is the silver or silver gilt trays and boxes of her dressing case which are the delight of the picture. They are rendered with an astonishing sheen and finish; while, in the silver looking glass, the Queen can be seen reflected in profile and looking very young. Behind her, against a mirror in the wall, two figures of china mandarins continue the exotic note, which is balanced, again, by the little Prince's drum, splendidly finished in bravura, and reposing upon the seat of an armchair in the corner. Outside, through the open window, a stork or flamingo casts its long shadow on the lawn. Finally, at the other side of the picture, by a tall French ormolu clock, which the loving care of her descendant, Queen Mary, has sought out and placed as near as possible to the portrait of itself, in the corridor at Windsor, Zoffany has painted an open door and an enfilade of rooms leading away into the distance and flooded with sunlight through their many windows. But, indeed, the whole picture is suffused with this happy sunlight. We can be certain that it would be thus, alone with her children, that Queen Charlotte would have herself remembered by posterity. She would be content, we may be sure, to see that picture of herself in her youth on such a summer day as this. It was not to be long before this little boy and girl, and their eleven brothers and sisters, grew into the quarrelling and unhappy Hanoverians of the Regency. But, of that, there is no hint in this unclouded summer, and the warm stillness is only waiting for a clock to strike, for a chime to sound and an exotic bird to sing.

This picture, as well it might, met with the approval of the King and Queen. A year or two before, Zoffany had painted the large group of George III and Queen Charlotte, with the six children already born to them, but all the portraits are in Van Dyck dress and it is a pompous and very unimpressive group. The King liked Zoffany because of his neatness and his pictures of the play, so that, having gained the Royal favour, he was able to embark upon the ambitious plan that now occurred to him. This came to fruition, however, after another and perhaps more interesting project had ended in nothing. It had been proposed that Zoffany should accompany Captain Cook on one of his voyages to the South Sea Islands. He was to be given every opportunity for his work and to have three draughtsmen as assistants under him. At the last moment this plan proved abortive, and Hodges, an artist of inferior talent, took the place of Zoffany on the expedition. But Zoffany had, by now, owing to his expensive habits, got into debt and was determined to leave England. He, therefore, acted upon a suggestion made by Queen Charlotte that he should make a journey to Italy and, while in Florence, make a sketch of the interior of the Uffizi. For this, he was to have his expenses paid and three hundred pounds a year. Zoffany arrived in Florence in the winter of 1772-3 and, at once, set to work.

The fact that he was armed with a Royal commission from George III gave full emphasis to his self-importance. Sir Horace Mann, the correspondent of Walpole, was then Minister to the Tuscan Court and Zoffany was introduced by him to the Grand Duke. He was granted all the facilities that he wished for in order to paint the interior of the Uffizi. He even obtained the assistance of the Grand Duke's servants in order to carry anything that he wanted out of the rest of the Uffizi into the Tribuna.

This was a room built early in the seventeenth century by Cardinal Leopoldo de Medici in order to house the finest treasures in the collection. Zoffany had them augmented, so to speak, by anything else that he liked; and then the serious business of the painting began. His scheme had grown more ambitious as it proceeded and was, now, to combine the merits of a Conversation Piece with that fidelity in the reproduction of other paintings in miniature which is the criterion of certain Flemish interiors that depict a gallery of pictures. This was a feat of virtuosity that can be met with frequently in Flemish painting. The Elder Teniers, for instance, had painted the picture gallery of the Archduke Leopold William, Governor of the Netherlands, in this manner, and his picture is still to be seen in the gallery at Brussels. There are similar pictures by Teniers at Munich, at Vienna and in the Prado. But Zoffany, as he proceeded, almost assumed airs of personal ownership over the Tribuna. On certain days the public was excluded from the room, so that, in the end, much comment was aroused; and this was exactly what Zoffany had intended.

Florence was, then, a point of interception for English travellers between Venice and Rome or Naples. It had, also, a permanent English colony presided over by Sir Horace Mann and including Lord Cowper and the painter, or caricaturist, Thomas Patch. Every wealthy young English-man going round on the Grand Tour came to Florence. Some twenty or twenty-five of these persons were included by Zoffany as portraits in the Tribuna; where, indeed, apart from himself, there are none but Englishmen present. As the painting progressed the personnel were continually changing. Another and more important Englishman would arrive, or his predecessor would in some manner annoy Zoffany and his portrait would be rubbed out to make way for the next comer. A painter of less persistence than Zoffany would never have finished the picture.

But, at last, this tour de force was completed (33). It had occupied the greater part of two years of the painter's life; and, indeed, it is hardly a picture. It is a peepshow, or a kaleidoscope in arrested motion. Both background and foreground are occupied with copies, or brilliant imitations of old masters, not in painting only, but antique sculpture. Into this welter of bric à brac, for even the floor is littered with antique vases, Zoffany has introduced his portraits of Sir Horace Mann, Lord Cowper, Thomas Patch, and all of the rich young Englishmen who passed through Florence at that time. In midst of them, for Zoffany had his racial instinct for business, he is to be seen, in person, exhibiting a Raphael Madonna which he had bought as a bargain. It was his own property and had nothing to do with the Uffizi. He is showing it, in the picture, to Lord Cowper, and to a purpose, for

Lord Cowper afterwards bought it and had it taken to England. The insertion of these twenty or twenty-five portraits into this already crowded picture was a triumph of juggling; but, in criticism, it is of no use to complain of the overcrowding of this picture, for that was precisely its point and purpose. It is, as we have said, hardly a picture at all; but it is certainly a Conversation Piece. It is, indeed, a conversation of the cognoscenti or dilettanti. Our only regret may be that, instead of Florence, which had ceased at that time to have any contemporary interest, Zoffany did not paint the interior of the Doge's Palace, at Venice.

While in Florence, Zoffany also found time to paint the fine group of Lord Cowper and his family (31), which picture is now the property of Lady Desborough. It was painted at the Villa Palmieri, Lord Cowper's home in Florence, and two of Lady Cowper's family are playing the 'cello and the harpsichord while Lord Cowper and his wife listen. There is a Venetian picture, perhaps a Pittoni, upon the wall, and in the background the wooded banks of the Arno. Except for the Tribuna, this is the most important of the pictures painted by Zoffany in Italy; but the painter had other ambitions to fulfil, and having been presented in Florence to the future Joseph II he proceeded to Vienna, passing, on the way, through Parma, where he must have painted the little picture of Wandering Musicians that has already been mentioned. In Vienna he painted more than one group of the Imperial family, but these are official portraits and not Conversation Pieces. More important still, he obtained for himself, from Maria Theresa, the patent of a Baron of the Holy Roman Empire. This was granted him on 4 December, 1776.

In 1779 Zoffany returned to London, bearing with him the Tribuna, which he hoped to sell to George III for one thousand guineas. But complaints rose on all sides that Zoffany had exceeded his commission and had made the picture ridiculous by introducing so many portraits for which no stipulation had been made. After much acrimonious discussion the picture was returned to his hands; but Queen Charlotte bought it, some years later, and the Tribuna still hangs, as we have said, in the Royal collection.

The influence of the Tribuna continued in him. This was made manifest in a passion for overcrowding, which reaches its culmination in the most important of the Conversation Pieces that he painted upon his return to England. We refer to the Sharp family, of 1781 (32). Whatever its shortcomings, this is one of the most ambitious of Zoffany's compositions. The Sharps were famed for their musical talent and, in the summer, when they lived at Fulham, gave concerts on the river. The Royal Family then occupied

John Zoffany

34.   THE AURIOL FAMILY

M. G. Dashwood, Esq.

John Zoffany

35. THE HEATLY GROUP

Captain C. D. M. Blunt

the Palace at Kew, and the river was the scene of much liveliness and serenading. Zoffany, himself, had a house at Strand-on-the-Green and a 'shallop' or barge on which he used to give concerts. According to Dr. G. C. Williamson, who had it on the authority of Mrs. Oldfield, a surviving grand-daughter of the painter, this 'shallop' was painted green, pink and drab, while the servants were put into a magnificent livery of scarlet and gold, with blue facings, the heraldic colours of the coat of arms that had been granted him by the Empress Maria Theresa, while on the shoulder knots occurred the Zoffany crest of a sprig of clover in silver between buffaloes' horns, rising out of a baron's coronet. The houseboat of the Sharps must have been, so to speak, the rival concern to that 'shallop' and its gaudy occupants. Zoffany has painted no fewer than fifteen persons on board of it, nearly all of whom are either singing or playing instruments. One of them holds a serpent, an instrument possessed of so many snakelike twists and convolutions that, had he been raising it to his lips to play, nearly every other portrait in the picture would have been obscured. The centre of the canvas is occupied by a harpsichord on which reposes a theorbo, a musical instrument which has a prophetic resemblance to an old fashioned or horned gramophone. It is, in fact, the sempiternal river party; and, in the back, the figures rise in a pyramid to the top of the canvas so that there is scarcely room for the flag which flies from the stern of the vessel. It is a noisy, crowded, unlovely composition, and cost its owners eight hundred guineas, a large sum of money for that day.

In little more than a year after this was painted Zoffany set sail for India. We, therefore, for the sake of clearness, reserve the discussion of his other Conversation Pieces until his return, for this will afford an opportunity to consider the best among them, at a time, and without interruption. Meanwhile his visit to India was productive of some charming Anglo Indian portrait groups which form a division to themselves in his work. In those days the permission of the East India Company had to be obtained before a person of no official standing could take up residence in their settlements. He arrived in India in September 1783 and proceeded, at once, to Lucknow where the Nawab of Oudh, Nasaf-ud-Daula, was the centre of the most extravagant native court in India. He was building in a bastard European style, part Hindu, part Gothic and part classical, in fact the gateways and pavilions of Lucknow were ancestors to Brighton Pavilion. During his stay in this city, Zoffany finished three large paintings representing a Tiger Hunt, a Cock Fight, and the Embassy of Hyderbeck to Calcutta from the Nawab of Oudh. All three of these are overcrowded and far from successful as pictures.

But, in contrast, there are the delightful Anglo Indian groups that Zoffany accomplished. Four of them, especially, take a very high rank in his achievement. These, at least, are the best of those known to us in the original, or by reproduction, but it may be regarded as certain that there are others, hardly inferior, which may come to light. He was in India, we must remember, for six years, a long period of time for a person of his industrious habits. Best of all, perhaps, is the Auriol group (34), now belonging to the Dashwood family, their descendants. It must have presented peculiar difficulties in composition, for there are seven portraits as well as native servants, but Zoffany has solved the problem by forming them into three subsidiary groups. The two ladies are seated at a table, under a tree, drinking tea; while the others are playing chess, or talking in a group. All the dresses worn are exceedingly bright and rich in colour, and the silver tea urn and porcelain cups and saucers are painted with all Zoffany's customary care and attention. The Impey group, still the property of the family, shows Sir Elijah Impey, the famous judge, with his children and servants. There are, in fact, ten Indian servants in the picture, including a musician in a white muslin dress who plays a kind of mandoline, and two ayahs who are seated on the ground playing with Sir Elijah's children.

It is even more pleasant to turn to another group which represents Mr. Suetonius Grant Heatly and his sister Temperance (35). This belongs to Captain Blunt, their collateral descendant. This time it is an interior. The cool bare wall of the room makes a foil for the exquisitely painted figure of Miss Temperance Heatly, and for the splendid turban and gold embroidered vest of the Indian servant who stands behind her brother, holding a hookah, or native tobacco pipe. Meanwhile, a grave and dignified Indian, bearded and white turbaned, leans his long staff against his chest, while with hands pressed together he bows and salaams to them, and makes some important announcement. The fourth of these Indian Conversation Pieces portrays for us that interesting character Colonel Martin, a French adventurer from Lyons who came out to Lucknow and made a high position for himself in the Nawab's court. He collected an immense fortune and built the Martinière, a palace in the bastard or Brighton style of Oudh. In it he is buried, in a tomb that is guarded by the statues of four grenadiers with reversed arms. Martin was a friend and patron of Zoffany. When he died, he left nineteen pictures and forty-five sketches by his hand; and there are still pictures by Zoffany in the Martinière, which is maintained as a school by the terms of Martin's will. In the picture we are now describing—it belongs to Mr. W. C. Bridgeman, M.P.—Colonel Martin is explaining the plans of the Martinière to Major Wombwell, while in the other corner

Colonel Polier, another adventurer and companion of Martin, is buying fruit from some Indians. In the background we see Zoffany himself, seated at his easel, and five of his pictures, none of them, we may add, of much interest, decorate the walls. This painting, which is said to be dated 1788, must be one of the last of those executed by Zoffany in India, for, little more than a year later, he returned to London, but unaccompanied by the fortune that had been his anticipation.

On the whole, his six years in India must be accounted a disappointment. The Heatly and Auriol groups are on the level of his best English Conversation Pieces; but Zoffany seems to have been unable to strike that exotic note which we should have expected of him. The portrait of Queen Charlotte and her two children has more of the exotic or poetic distance than anything that he achieved in India. With his innate talent for self-identification he becomes, not the artist visiting a strange land, but the Anglo Indian official trying to reproduce the conditions of home in a hated exile. In the Auriol group, Zoffany suddenly remembers he is in India and inserts a crooked palm tree, like the neck of a long giraffe or sea serpent, into the conventional trees that are his background and that recall the English scene. There is, in fact, no evidence that he made a special study of his new surroundings. And yet, in certain single portraits of Indians, in his picture of the Nawab of Oudh (Lord Tweedmouth), in his portrait of Rao Sindhia that is still preserved in a little pagoda near Poona, or in that of Benaram Pundit, which belonged to Warren Hastings, his direct or personal observation has resulted in portraits that are in no way to be distinguished from paintings by competent native artists. They are, in fact, the wooden or uninspired image; and, of this, the Indians, too, are capable.

As soon as he came back to London the thoughts of Zoffany must have returned to his other triumphal homecoming, from Italy, with the Tribuna. It was essential that he should paint a picture of outstanding merit in order to court attention, once more. And the opportunity came to him in the very form, indeed, of the Tribuna. Charles Towneley, the famous collector of antiques, commissioned him to paint a group of himself and his friends in conversation and surrounded by the marbles. This picture of the Towneley marbles (37) is now the property of Lord O'Hagan, who is descended from the collector. The home of the Towneley family was in Lancashire; but Charles Towneley had taken a house at 7 Park Street, now 14 Queen Anne's Gate. In painting this picture, Zoffany followed his precedent at the Uffizi and had any objects that he wanted to represent carried from all parts of the house into the inner hall or library. This room is, or was recently, in existence, and it is said that the painter has much exaggerated its dimensions, which could not possibly have held this crowd of statues and bas reliefs, while allowing room, as well, for the free circulation of their owner and his three friends who are painted with him. It is, however, not only interesting and successful as a picture but a commentary on the history of taste; for, without exception, none of the Greco Roman objects here assembled, most of which are now in the British Museum, would have any value in the eyes of a present day collector. The house of Mr. Eumorfopoulos, before its contents were bought by the nation, will give us the contrast we are searching for between the taste of Towneley and the taste of our own times. The Towneley marbles are like one of the interiors of the Soane Museum; but, at least, Towneley and his like had still a hold over the taste of their own times. There were great architects and craftsmen living. Now, there are none.

For the remainder of Zoffany's life, lasting for another twenty years until 1810, we make no attempt at a chronological survey of his activity. His best work was done, and his last exhibit at the Royal Academy was in 1800. Instead, we return to the plethora of his portrait groups, painted, some few of them, during these last years, but dating, for the most part, from his return to London from Italy, or even from before his departure to Florence. This method has the merit of enabling us to discuss the best of them, together and at a time, putting in the dates, when necessary, and not distracting the text with numbers.

A few of his Conversation Pieces call for immediate mention, at this moment. They are the two groups of Garrick and his wife (38, 39); the Dutton picture (29); and the portrait of Lord Willoughby de Broke and his family (44). Zoffany never painted better pictures than these; and no history of eighteenth century art is complete without them. But the importance of the English Conversation Piece, which is not yet recognized abroad, except in America, has not attached enough interest to itself for the merit of a first rate Zoffany or a Stubbs to be accorded the international fame that it deserves. The dictionaries of paintings are, indeed, still careful of their space where Zoffany is concerned. Also, there are not yet enough Zoffanys in picture galleries, and his finest works, as is the case with every English painter of the school, still repose in country houses, which is as it should be, but is uninstructive for the public. With the two pictures, for instance, of Garrick and his wife, it is difficult to arrive at any comparison of their merit as works of art. Their rank, we may assume, is about that of the pair of pictures by Bellotto in the Liechtenstein Gallery at Vienna. Those are, in fact, Conversation Pieces, taken in the gardens of that palace. They are

John Zoffany

National Gallery, London

36.   A FAMILY GROUP

37.   CHARLES TOWNELEY WITH HIS FRIENDS IN HIS LIBRARY

John Zoffany

Lord O'Hagan

universally admired; but the Zoffanys in question are hardly known still and have only, lately, made their appearance at one or two recent exhibitions.

The first of them represents Mr. and Mrs. Garrick on the steps of the temple that Garrick built to the memory of Shakespeare, on the banks of the Thames, near Hampton Court (39). The river sweeps along in the picture; and its imminence is, somehow, made more apparent, still, by the thinness and newness of the temple. The colour note of the dresses is blue. Mrs. Garrick is dressed entirely in that colour; while her husband has blue breeches, a long blue vest and a white surcoat. In the front of the picture, an immense St. Bernard dog is lying on the smooth scythed grass. A weeping willow, like long flowing hair, grows on the river bank and drips into the flowing water.

The companion picture (38) shows a smooth expanse, or lawn of grass, that sweeps down to the river. A mahogany table is set upon this; and, at it, are grouped Mr. and Mrs. Garrick, another friend of theirs, and no less a figure than Mr. Bowden. It has been recently ascertained that the figure on the left is this Mr. Bowden and not Dr. Johnson, as stated on the title of Fig. 38. Garrick, himself, is the man standing up behind the table. In the foreground, a small dog is guarding a three cornered hat that lies upon the grass. George Garrick, the actor's brother, is to be seen with his fishing rod, throwing into the river. Most of his figure shows against the water and is focus for the wide and spreading river scene that meanders into the distance. Another weeping willow, the beginning of romanticism, rises behind him and the garden ends in a whole grove of willows, flowing down with green tresses into the stream. The water is painted without a ripple and flows away towards far-off London, past the villa'ed banks and by a wooded eyot. It is, in fact, the unmistakable but early Thames, rendered in the picture as in the aquatints of William Havell, with grazing cattle on the low banks of the other side and a barge crawling painfully and slowly up the current. Round the next bend there will be the red and white palace of Hampton Court, its Wren façades, its cipher stones of William and Mary, the clipped hedges and the Tijou gates. In both of these pictures we have a summer day by the river from the hand of one who lived but a little distance further down its banks. A hot June day at Hampton Court, which must be a living memory to many thousands of men and women, is continued into this sylvan shade, near by, with its Palladian temple. This pair of pictures becomes part of the long tradition of the Thames. The carved and gilded pleasure barges of the Rape of the Lock, drift along the stream; we hear the hornpipe of Handel's Water Music; and come to the poet's shell grotto and the Gothick battlements of Strawberry Hill. Such is the river, from the spires of Oxford and the hanging woods of Marlow, down past the villas till the dome of St. Paul's comes into view, the limewhite formal Greenwich and the crowded pool, with sails set for China and the Indies. This pair of pictures are evocative of that; but Zoffany has painted them with no emphasis, even on the weather. It is a hot day, the average of the summer; and his fine sense of comedy, so often seen in his pictures of the theatre, has treated Dr. Johnson with reverence and dignity. His figure is not in the least characterized. And the great actor, in both pictures, has no part to play. All is in proportion to the pleasant scene, the chiming water and the willow trees.

It is a convincing proof of the powers of Zoffany to turn from these pictures of the Thames to one of the best interior scenes that he ever painted. This is the portrait group of the Dutton family (29). It portrays an old father and mother and their grown-up son and daughter. The son became, in later years, Lord Sherborne and his sister married the Earl of Leicester, and lived at Holkham. They are depicted in the typical surroundings of that age of taste; but the rendering is inimitable. The plot of the picture is a card table; but the old lady sits away from it, in order to warm herself at the fire. Her son is showing her his hand and asking what card to play. She has put down her book upon her lap to answer him; while, at the far side of the table, the father and daughter wait impatiently and resent the interruption. The picture is full of delightful passages of painting. The blue chair, studded with brass nails, on which Miss Dutton is sitting is so beautifully rendered that it recalls, for a moment, that miraculous blue sofa on which Mme Manet is lying in the pastel at the Louvre. The sensation of this blue chair can be compared to a master hand playing a glissando or a rippling scale. But there is, also, the carpet, a Persian rug which is painted with a delightful and complicated dexterity. And a marble mantelpiece, of that sort which is one of the glories of English houses, a little earlier than Adam in design, and with several small bronze ornaments upon it, of Pompeian taste and in the style of Pergolese. Everything is in place and given its due importance and no more. Such perfect proportion of parts is only to be met with elsewhere in the chamber music of Mozart. This picture, indeed, might be compared to a piano quartet of Mozart. It has the same loveliness of truth and unimportance; no more, in this instance, than a game of cards, but giving a held moment or a permanence of life. It is the truth of a living moment, in the flashing colours with which time passes by, unnoticed. This is, indeed, the Conversation Piece in the height of its achievement, for the secret of that is realism through informality.

38. THE GARRICKS ENTERTAINING DR. JOHNSON

John Zoffany

The Earl of Durham

39. MR. AND MRS. GARRICK AT SHAKESPEARE'S TEMPLE AT HAMPTON

John Zoffany

The Earl of Durham

John Zoffany

40.   THE COLMORE FAMILY

Sir Philip Sassoon, Bart.

41.   CAPTAIN HERVEY TAKING LEAVE OF HIS FAMILY

John Zoffany

The Marquess of Bristol

42. A MAN AND TWO BOYS, ONE WITH A KITE

John Zoffany   *Sir Sidney Herbert, Bart.*

43. MR. AND MRS. BLEW AND FAMILY

John Zoffany   *Lady Hudson*

44. LORD WILLOUGHBY DE BROKE AND HIS FAMILY

But the group of Lord Willoughby de Broke and his family (44) is no less successful. This, also, is an interior scene, and its subject consists of a father and mother and three small children. The setting is somewhat similar to that of the Dutton group. Again there is a marble mantelpiece and a splendid Turkey rug upon the floor. Lord Willoughby de Broke is leaning over the back of his wife's chair, shaking his finger at one of the little girls who is helping herself to a slice of buttered toast from the tea tray. His wife is wearing a beautifully painted blue dress and holds the baby in her arms, while the third child plays with a red, wooden horse. But the most delightful passage in the picture is the silver urn of Adam's design, still in possession of the family, and a delicately painted porcelain tea service, with all the light and shine of china. In this picture, also, there is the harmony of perfect proportion, alike in incident and in accessory.

These two groups represent the Conversation Piece in its maturity and at a height of achievement beyond which it never advanced. It is to be noticed that, by this time, the type has entirely established itself. In the hands of Hogarth some plot had to be unfolded or a convenient excuse must present itself for the assembly of so many figures. This makes a good Hogarth Conversation Piece into something of a tour de force, and its repetition at the same level of accomplishment cannot be expected to occur more than a few times. With Hogarth it happened some six or eight times, but Zoffany has so enlarged the boundaries that nearly every group he undertakes becomes an opportunity that he cannot neglect. We have only to consider the Dutton group and the Willoughby family, in contrast with the two Garrick groups, or with the portrait of Queen Charlotte and her two elder children, in order to realize the advance wrought by Zoffany in this art to which he devoted his energies. Also, the Dutch ancestry of the Conversation Piece, its derivation from de Hoogh, or Mieris, or Metsu, is no longer apparent. It has become an absolutely English creation, instinct with the English reserve and subordination. The group that was last described could, by no possibility, be otherwise than English in its origin.

Zoffany at his best is to be admired in the portrait group belonging to Lady Hudson (43). This represents a gentleman playing the flute, his wife and two little daughters. The picture relates itself more particularly to the Minuet of the Glasgow Gallery. We shall arrive at that in a moment. It is a Zoffany, that is to say, which is suggestive of John Raphael Smith. We know that Zoffany was a very musical man; and it is amusing in this picture to see the Apollo-like pose of the gentleman, an antique statue as to his limbs, but clothed in all the finery of the late eighteenth century. This flute player, who is playing, perhaps, one of the flute sonatas of Handel, gives to the picture an interest to which the more ordinary subjects of Zoffany cannot aspire.

Even now, many fine groups by Zoffany call for notice. There are the two portraits of the Drummond family. In the first, we see Mr. Andrew Drummond, the founder of the famous Bank, seated under a tree, with his children and grandchildren gathered round him. Two of them are riding on ponies. In the second picture, another branch of the same family, being this old gentleman's nephew and his descendants, are painted at Cadland, with a view over the Solent towards the Isle of Wight (45). This is, perhaps, the more interesting of the two groups, because of the wider freedom of the grouping, because of the six charming small boys portrayed in it, and for the sailing ships, down in the distance, making with their white wings for Portsmouth or Southampton. But, in both pictures, there is a hint of the limitations of Zoffany's art, for the trees are in no wise different from that under which the Auriol family reposed, in far-off India. Zoffany, it is clear, had little or no feeling for nature. He could paint the weeping willows of the river bank, but wild or exotic nature was not his bent.

Another group which invites comparison with the foregoing is that of Captain Hervey taking leave of his family on his appointment to the command of a ship (41). This still belongs to his descendant, the Marquess of Bristol. The family are sitting under a pillared portico, against which the waves are lapping. A dinghy is drawn up, and Captain Hervey, who occupies the open foreground, is about to turn round and step into it, bound for his vessel, which lies at anchor in the open roadstead, showing its carved and gilded stern.

A more formal painting represents the family of Sir William Young, and is now the property of Sir Philip Sassoon (46). The family, who are eleven in number, are grouped at the foot of a flight of steps. They are all in Van Dyck dress and Sir William and his wife are playing, respectively, a violoncello and a mandoline or lute. But this picture is an alternative to the group of Anglo Indian nabobs and their families, for Sir William was a West Indian magnate, being Governor of the islands of St. Vincent and Dominica. For this reason a negro servant occurs in the picture, where he holds a little child on horseback on the lap of its elder brother. And the same negro comes into another picture by Zoffany, which is, indeed, just a replica of that portion or corner of the bigger painting. There is, also, a charming group by Zoffany of one of the sons and his sister, an adaptation, also, from the larger canvas; and this son was, in his time, Governor of Tobago and owner, we may presume, of many negro slaves.

John Zoffany 45. THE DRUMMOND FAMILY AT CADLAND *The Hon. Mrs. Iomides*

46.   THE FAMILY OF SIR WILLIAM YOUNG

Sir Philip Sassoon possesses, as well, the Colmore family (40), an excellent outdoor specimen of Zoffany in the height of his powers. There is a delightful old lady in this picture holding her grandchild, and three other little children are painted with all Zoffany's skill in depicting the very young. In the foreground there is a splendid bantam hen with its chickens, the pride, it is certain, of the children in the picture. This canvas might be described as a Zoffany above the average, but not one of his masterpieces.

This word must be reserved, however, for the next picture here mentioned. It is the Minuet, now hanging in the Glasgow Gallery (50). This occupies a place, apart, in Zoffany's work. A little boy and a young girl are learning the minuet, while the mother and father watch them and another man plays the flute. The background is left bare, and all the interest centres upon the turn and movement of the daughter. Dr. Williamson mentions the influence of Watteau upon this picture; but it would be more accurate to suggest that exquisite painter Henry Walton, or the engraver John Raphael Smith, whose rare original designs have this same quality of freshness and this rounding of the shape and body. It is, in fact, of John Raphael Smith that this picture is suggestive; and were it not signed (if it is?) some doubt might even be cast upon its ascription to Zoffany. But, as a Zoffany it stands; and, if considered as such, fills a unique and important place in his painting.

There could be no greater contrast than between the preceding and the pair of paintings that belong to the Marquess of Bute (49, 48); the first of them represents the daughters of the family playing under the branches of a tree. The entrance to a fine Palladian stables is to be seen in the background. The second shows three little boys playing, likewise, in a tree. One of these boys grew into the Archbishop of Armagh and was Primate of Ireland. Another painting of children shows us a father and his two sons who are flying a kite. This is certainly among the most charming of Zoffanys (42). And we have left, till last, another group of a father and mother with five children and what would seem to be a little black boy kneeling in the corner (36); and, to conclude with, the large and important group of Zoffany, himself, as an old man, with his children and descendants (51). And, even now, there remains to be mentioned the group of the Richardson family, in the National Gallery at Dublin, a picture predominantly green in colour, of green clothes, green lawns, a fir tree and a weeping willow.

It is probable that the greater part of his important pictures have now been mentioned by us in some detail. But the output of Zoffany was so large and varied that there can be no certainty as to the omissions. It is always possible that another group may come to light which is as fine as the Dutton or the Willoughby paintings. There must be pictures, hidden away and ignored, which a judicious cleaning will restore to their author.

A picture by Zoffany, which is the equal, in some ways, of those two Conversation Pieces just mentioned, is in the collection of the Marquess of Zetland. It represents the first Lord Zetland with his grandfather, Sir Lawrence Dundas (47). The interest of this painting lies in the amazing fidelity of the interior, which is a marvel of tact and technical skill. The old gentleman, in his white wig, is sitting in the centre of the canvas but a long way back at the far end of the room and in front of a splendid and typical mantelpiece. The tables and empty chairs have the interest, almost, of living persons, for their character dominates the scene and the empty room. Their cubical or spatial drama fills the void and has given the painter an opportunity to exercise his matchless skill upon their angles of perspective and their satiny or mahogany sheen. The Turkey carpet, as often before, is a feat of virtuosity in itself. But the mantelshelf is adorned with seven bronze groups in Greco Roman taste upon which Zoffany has lavished his skill in counterfeit; while, above them and on each side of the wall, a collection of Dutch masters is represented with unerring fidelity. In particular, the big painting over the mantelpiece, which must be a shipping scene by Van der Capelle, is a quite extraordinary performance. This picture has qualities which entitle it to consideration with the Towneley marbles. Like that picture, it is hardly a portrait; but, indeed, this amount of detail would distract attention in the best of those portrait groups that we have described. It is an interior of live objects and inanimate persons.

It should now be possible, in the light of all that has been described, to attempt a general, and not particular, assessment of the art of Zoffany. In his own time his reputation depended to a like extent upon his theatrical pictures. Walpole says of him, 'Zoffany is delightful in his real way, and introduced the furniture of a room with great propriety: but his talent is neither for rooms simply, nor portraits. He makes wretched pictures when he is serious. His talent is to draw scenes in comedy, and there he beats the Flemish painters in their own way of detail.' Such pictures by him, of which the best collection is, of course, that of the Garrick Club, are not our present concern. But they formed, at least, his school of life. Perhaps no painter, who was not an addict of the theatre, could have grouped his figures so readily and with such ease. Hogarth, also, it will be remembered, drew from the stage. Perhaps the theatre, in the art of the Conversation Piece, occupied the same place as the nude in any school of historical painting. The study of it was essential to success. The continual grouping and posing of the actors was their perpetual display of subject. Nowhere

40

John Zoffany

47.   SIR LAWRENCE DUNDAS WITH HIS GRANDSON, LAWRENCE

The Marquess of Zetland

48.   THE SONS OF JOHN, THIRD EARL OF BUTE

John Zoffany   *The Marquess of Bute*

49.   THE DAUGHTERS OF JOHN, THIRD EARL OF BUTE

John Zoffany   *The Marquess of Bute*

else could it be studied to such advantage, as while you sat in darkness and silence looking at the peepshow.

Garrick and his school acted against a background of realism. Zoffany in his picture of Garrick as Abel Drugger, one of the very finest of his theatrical subjects, shows us the detailed background with all the alchemist's properties; the globe, the skull, the hourglass, the embryo in spirit in its bottle, the stuffed body of the bat nailed to the wall. These are real and not painted upon the scene. They are like a Teniers painting of a hermit in his cell. Walpole says, that 'it is one of the best pictures ever done by this Genius.' The still life is painted as carefully as in the Tribuna or the Towneley marbles. This is, therefore, the antithesis of what might be expected of a theatrical picture. Another of these subjects, the scene from 'Speculation,' at the Garrick Club, shows Quick, the famous comedian, in a setting which is as static as that of the Dutton group. It is only lowered into comedy by the large stomach and burlesqued wig of Quick, helped by the portrait of himself over the mantelpiece, and, otherwise, might pass for a family group, an uncle and two nephews, perhaps, in dispute over some escapade of one of the younger men. This is, in fact, the natural or du Maurier school of acting where every detail is designed to make the spectator feel at home. Also, the picture in question is a late one, dating from 1795, and Zoffany has abandoned the Flemish influence which is so conspicuous in that painting of Garrick as Abel Drugger.

The other method of approaching the theatrical scene is to be studied in the picture of Mrs. Siddons, as Lady Macbeth, by Henry Fuseli. This painting, which was exhibited in London, last year, after long neglect, has that momentary, that flickering reality which is the truth of an impression, of a shock of horror. In form, it is an apparition, and hardly human in its shape. But it sends a swifter message to the senses than does the detailed approach of Zoffany. Fuseli was an artist of morbid imagination and nightmare fancy, with a gift that rose, at times, into a region that had scarcely before been traversed. But Zoffany, by contrast, could never transcend the truth. At the same time, his patience let him, nearly always, achieve it. Fuseli could not be relied upon, for his technique was deficient except in moments of inspiration, and his fancy might not get to work. Yet, in this picture of Lady Macbeth, there is more aesthetic pleasure to be had from the impetuous fury of his paint than in the finish and glossiness of Zoffany. Fuseli composed out of his imagination: Zoffany had wonderful vision, but no fancy.

If patience is stressed as one of the virtues of this painter it is not only the Dutch or Flemish detail that is intended. When a Conversation Piece with some eight or ten portraits was on hand, the progress of the painting had to be postponed from month to month, until occasion offered. The group had to be painted in, portrait by portrait, when each subject was available. We give a drawing, attributed to Zoffany, in which some half-dozen persons are seated or standing round a table (97). The drawing is of interest, in itself, as showing the slow and careful process by which the Conversation Piece had to be built up character by character. It can be seen that each individual person has been separately studied, sitting at the table, and perhaps the largeness of the hands, which is a defect in the drawing, is a sign of this fatigue and monotony of study. These very criticisms will serve to show the tedious processes through which the Conversation Piece had to pass before it could take on its qualities of vitality and truth to nature. This drawing, in all probability, is but a preliminary and careful study of likenesses, before the arrangement of the figures was undertaken. And, when their places had been allotted to them, there would remain, in the case of Zoffany, the painstaking rendering of every accessory and detail. An important picture of this nature will have occupied many months of toil.

The pictures of the Young or the Auriol families must have involved innumerable separate sittings, and constant alteration. The fitting in of so many living individuals into the crowded floor of the Tribuna, and the disposition of their portraits in such wise as not to obscure the masterpieces upon the walls, was no less than a marvel of ingenuity. It is a Diploma picture, another Derby Day, and worthy, indeed, of the despised Frith. But Zoffany, at least, could subordinate truth to effect and did not insist upon the harsh hardness of every living or dead entity. His effects of Flemish detail were done in order to convey the truth, and not to impose it like the terms of a conquering enemy. We have the impression that Frith, had it been possible, would have painted the back as well as the front of his canvas. But Zoffany, from his knowledge of the theatre, knew where the scene must end.

His portrait groups have the proper limits of the Conversation Piece. There are instances, as in the Zetland group, where he has painted the room more than the persons contained in it, but this is his dramatization of empty chairs. The whole effect of the picture lies in the stillness of the old man and his grandchild in midst of so many objects that catch and hold the attention. Other of his pictures, the Heatly group or the Minuet, have a blank wall for background, but this dictates a deeper concentration of interest upon the figures. If it is movement, in the Minuet, or the strangeness and sparkle of the Oriental costume, this scenic emptiness justifies itself and adds drama to the portraits. But a long line of figures, eight or ten or more members of a family, cannot be sufficiently individualized where there are no palliating interests in the background and no drama among the numbers. In such paintings, therefore, as the Auriol group, Zoffany has invented three separate actions, chess playing, tea drinking and simple conversation, and the serpentine line of those eleven figures unwinds and unravels itself along the foreground. The Young group contains no less than twelve portraits and, here again, the composition is divided into three divisions or departments. They are grouped round a horse, on the left; in the centre they play musical instruments; and, on the right, the flight of stone steps provides a pedestal and lifts the figures to a height that balances the equestrian group upon the other side.

But, on the whole, it was when Zoffany worked within the strictest limits that he achieved the most success. A Conversation properly called, cannot consist of more than four or five persons, and these requirements of the Riot Act fall most conveniently upon his two or three masterpieces in which that requisite number of persons provide the plot. The Dutton group, the Willoughby group, the picture of Queen Charlotte and her two elder children, these are his paintings in which perfect harmony and proportion have been attained. Proportion of accent in the detail, and harmony of every object, animate and inanimate, make these pictures into the image or simulacrum of life. The pictures hang upon the walls of the room, and the persons painted have their backs to them and pay no attention to those accepted accompaniments to their lives. Those pictures have the quiet and steady presence that is there all the time and that only comes into prominence when any particular notice is taken. They do not force themselves upon the attention; and yet their absence would be immediately apparent. In this way the average truth in the lives of his subjects has been attained. If it was exaggerated it would not be true. They must not even concentrate to a forced extent upon what they are doing. They must know that they are being painted. It is only the children who are likely to forget this and be natural.

If Zoffany is the painter who produced more Conversation Pieces than any other artist of the school he must, at the same time, be ever inferior to Gainsborough and Reynolds. Gainsborough had a greater gift for painting and was an Englishman, born and bred. Reynolds, whom it is an affectation, now, to despise, was, perhaps, the only one of our painters who had the power of composition on the great and classical scale. He is the only English old master, while Gainsborough had too much talent and vitality for that. The astonishing start of Lawrence's career, and even the set of portraits painted, towards the end of his life, for the Waterloo Chamber at Windsor, put him upon a scale of achievement from which it could not be expected that he would stoop to the trivial but delightful detail which is characteristic of the Conversation Piece. It might be said, indeed, that the array of Lawrences in the Waterloo Chamber are the last full dress flowering of official art anywhere in European painting. Since then, it has been a rebel art and has been denied official employment.

A more useful comparison can be drawn between Zoffany and the minor, or secondary, painters. The essence of the Conversation Piece is its intimacy, and it is useless to expect this in connection with the greatest names of the period. Before, therefore, we come to compare Zoffany with the other artists of his own school it is instructive to contrast him with those painters who are his true equivalent. Zoffany was born in Germany, it is important to remember, and only came to England when he was between twenty-five and thirty years of age. The two painters with whom he can most aptly be compared are Jean Liotard (1702-1779) and Raphael Mengs (1728-1779). Liotard was a native of Geneva, while Mengs was a Saxon, born at Dresden. Both of them are international painters and, like Zoffany, sought their fortunes abroad. Liotard, as is well known, lived for many years in Constantinople and, in order to attract attention to himself on his return home, grew a long beard and wore the flowing Oriental dress. He worked for considerable periods in Paris, in London and in Holland. 'La Belle Chocolatière,' his best known work in gouache, is in the Dresden Gallery, and this picture, as we have pointed out, has a strong technical resemblance to the little picture by Zoffany in the gallery at Parma. There is, also, an excellent group of Liotards in the Rijksmuseum at Amsterdam. Among these, a hint of Ingres, or of Degas, attaches to the portrait of Lady Coventry in Turkish dress. Liotard had the same love of painting porcelain cups and saucers as had Zoffany, and the same German or snow reflected lighting of his subjects. But it must be said that Liotard drew more inspiration from his residence in the East than did Zoffany from the six years that he spent in India. The style of Liotard was founded entirely upon his Eastern experiences; while Zoffany painted, in India, precisely as he would have done in London, with the exception of those one or two native portraits which are as stiff and wooden as if they were the work of an inferior Rajput painter. Liotard has the clear blues and whites of china tiles, and, for his dresses, the stiff or formal Brusa flower patterns, the convention of the Rhodian plate, the cypress and the rose, the tulip and the pink. His odalisques, in the elaborate coiffing of their silken turbans, are forerunners of the Grande Odalisque of Ingres. They wear wide trousers of silk and

44

walk on high pattens, while their finger tips and the palms of their hands are dyed with vermilion. Liotard was a miniaturist and should have painted no larger than a pane of glass.

Raphael Mengs, in contrast, is only comparable to Zoffany in one phase of his work. His heroic paintings are failures and, in pastel, he is inferior to Rosalba. But his portraits have certain points in common with Zoffany, more especially in the painting of Queen Charlotte and her two elder children. It is necessary to have visited Madrid in order to appreciate the portraits of Mengs. After having seen his pictures in the Prado, and in the former Royal Palace, it is, then, demonstrable that Mengs was the foremost portrait painter in costume of the eighteenth century. This is an aspect of his art which has been entirely neglected. There are portraits by him in the Royal Palace at Madrid which would produce a sensation, if exhibited together. Their quality is precisely that of the Zoffany in question. That painter would seem, on this occasion only, to have risen out of exactitude into fantasy. The chiming of musical boxes and the warbling of exotic birds in their cages of gilded wire come down the enfilade of rooms. After thinking of this picture, it is in the same breath that we can read, in Beckford's Letters from Italy and Spain, of his visit to this palace, in 1787, during the absence of the King. 'In every room we passed through stood cages of gilded wire, and in every cage a curious exotic bird in full song. Mingled with these warblings was heard, at certain intervals, the low chimes of musical clocks, stealing upon the ear like the tones of harmonic glasses. No other sound broke in upon the stillness except, indeed, the almost inaudible footsteps of several aged domestics, in court dresses of the cut and fashion prevalent in the days of the King's mother, Elizabeth Farnese, gliding along cautiously and quietly to open the cages and offer their inmates dainties such as highly educated birds should relish.'

Mengs, on the other hand, is no painter of Conversation Pieces. The comparison between himself and Zoffany is based upon their German finery of detail. The blue silk dress of Lady Willoughby de Broke is another passage which is reminiscent of Mengs. These similarities in their art are undeniably German. There are episodes in Zoffany's painting of the Tribuna, or the Towneley marbles, which are comparable to illustrations by Menzel of the life of Frederick the Great. He is to be compared in this to Menzel, and, as we have said, to Frith. If we revert, once more, to Raphael Mengs, it is because the portraits by Zoffany of the Hapsburg family, in the Vienna Gallery, could be mistaken for Mengs. It is evident that Zoffany was a conscious stylist, who could suit his manner to the subjects upon which he was employed. This was his racial advantage, for impersonation, or interpretation, is the talent of the Jews. When he was in Parma, or in Vienna, he could paint differently from what was expected of him in London. The small effect made upon him by his residence in India is another proof of this, for he was surrounded, there, by Englishmen more typical of their country than any to be found in London. He did not need to change; for, long ago, he had struck the note which was correct with them.

The basis of this was Hogarth. It was the cleverness of Zoffany to build upon it a structure, capable of endless variation. But Hogarth was a man of brusque humour. His character could not suit him for the career of a portrait painter. The ostentation of Zoffany, as we know from the exaggerated liveries of his servants, shows his love of fine living. It was his ambition to be on good terms, and to appear to advantage, as a Baron; or, as when, on his voyage to India, he assumed a knighthood for himself and took the title of Sir John Zoffany. In nothing is he more different from Hogarth than in this trait of character. Over this, and in his conduct in Florence, during the painting of the Tribuna, there is something of the travelling charlatan. They are the professionals of personal contact and an audience is their permanent necessity. The craft of Zoffany as a taker of likenesses, or limner of portraits, had this same perpetual need. But his strong theatrical leanings led him to interpret his sitters in exactly that atmosphere which was characteristic of them and most agreeable to themselves. It comes about, therefore, that the most typical pictures of the English were painted by a foreigner who never came to England until his twenty-seventh year. He adopted their latent style, the beginnings of which had their foundation in Hogarth, who was our first painter, and developed the early hints of this into a perfected form in which its origins are nearly lost to view. The hand of Hogarth is hardly to be seen in the Dutton group. It is no longer necessary for there to be a powerful and dramatic excuse for a picture. The Conversation Piece is, at last, conversation and no more than that.

Once it has been established that Zoffany was a foreigner working in London the truth of his stature as a painter will admit of explanation. He was a foreigner, here, like Liotard in London, or Raphael Mengs in Spain. It is, therefore, the more extraordinary that his paintings should admit of a direct comparison with Hogarth or with Stubbs. He contrived, indeed, to eject from English painting that Dutch influence which still shows to a certain extent in Hogarth. Under his hands the Conversation Piece freed itself from every extraneous derivation and became the picture of English life. This was a process which was undergoing development by other contemporary painters; but it was only Zoffany who devoted himself, nearly entirely, to these ends. Zoffany is the painter of the Conversation Piece, where other men only produced an occasional picture of this nature. Stubbs was an equine painter; and Copley, a painter of large historical subjects and single portraits. And yet it is to be recognized that, in their rare instances, these men were the equal of Zoffany. The one or two good pictures by Copley that come into this category are close rivals, even to the Dutton or Willoughby de Broke groups. What we should term Zoffany's 'diploma' paintings, the Tribuna or the Towneley marbles, are, though, more remarkable performances in every respect than the Death of Major Peirson or the Death of Chatham. But the comparison between Stubbs and Zoffany is not so quickly defined. Stubbs painted groups or Conversation Pieces which have all the quality of Zoffany's outdoor scenes, with something added. A solidity, a deeper and more masculine poetry, a superior skill in landscape, these are factors that make Stubbs a serious rival to Zoffany. And, where his own art is concerned, in equine painting, the astonishing friezes of horses that he painted at Wentworth Woodhouse have a power and a primal force which isolates them from the triviality of the eighteenth century and throws aspersions upon the laborious and jigsaw achievement of Zoffany in the Tribuna or the Towneley marbles. Stubbs is, in fact, a painter whom it is dangerous to compare too nearly to Zoffany, for he comes out of his obscurity to rival with him.

In the exterior scene, Zoffany is approached or surpassed by Stubbs; while Copley comes so near to Zoffany as to be indistinguishable in scale and achievement. There is, perhaps, little or nothing to choose between the Sitwell family by Copley and the Willoughby de Broke group by Zoffany; unless, indeed, the passages of still life in the latter picture, the triumph of the porcelain tea service and the silver tea urn, give this painting an advantage in solid handling over the brilliance with which Copley has painted the shuffled cards in the former picture. These are, most conspicuously, pictures of a school. The type has been defined and is beginning to be multiplied. This is the impression that is to be obtained when a number of Conversation Pieces are put upon exhibition. Zoffany and Copley, Stubbs and Devis, have painted this theme in every conceivable variation; while there are many other painters, with unknown names, who are little inferior in achievement. The exhibition of six years ago, in the house of Sir Philip Sassoon, was no less than a plethora of conscientious and delightful painting. The ubiquitous Zoffany had almost an exhibition to himself, so numerous were his pictures. Known and unknown painters nearly rivalled with him at every turn; but there was always another Zoffany to reassert his fame, and his repeated successes, if only by a narrow margin, could leave no doubt as to his predominance.

47

Zoffany, in every sense of its meaning, is the painter of the Conversation Piece. This is a kind of painting, of which the delight is, in part, its unimportance and remoteness. The mere fact that it is so far removed from the clash and crisis of life makes of it a comforting pleasure in our time. It has the calm and reserve which is characteristic of our art, and which is true of Wren, or Gibbs, or Adam, as it is of Gainsborough, or Constable, or Zoffany. And, in the same way that the achievement of a lesser man, of a Gibbs, compared with Wren or Adam, is in no disparagement of what he accomplished, so the inclusion of Zoffany in the same sentence as such names as those of Gainsborough or Constable is the true measure of his consistent craftsmanship. Zoffany is one of the creators of that happy century who seldom, if ever, disappoint their admirers. The same degree of delight that you may expect from a quartet by Haydn, from a sonata by Scarlatti, from a piece of Chelsea or of Meissen, from a room by Wyatt or Henry Holland, a façade by Gabriel or Héré, from a painting by Canaletto or Pietro Longhi, you may count upon procuring from a Conversation Piece by Zoffany. His name is the assurance of his achievement.

In the course of his long life of painting Zoffany kept to the accepted tenets of his time and did not dabble in romanticism. The turn of the century, with its wind of the Revolution, did not affect him. Neither is there a trace, in any of his paintings, of the craze for mediaevalism, for the sham Gothick, which was to destroy, in turn, every art but that of music and of fiction. None of the strain of Fuseli is apparent in Zoffany. Nor is there any hint of David and the Golden Age. Everything, in Zoffany, points to his contentment in his own time. It was, in a sense, the continuous present that he painted. He did not hanker after the past, or yearn for the future. The continuous present he prolonged, so that it still persists when we look upon his pictures. He has captured the illusion of life; and the phases of this pass by and perish even more quickly than do the illusions of the theatre, which are, at least, repeated in verisimilitude every evening. His love of the play, it has been suggested, was his school of life. This was the mirror in which he caught the gestures and attitudes of the living. But, unlike Hogarth, he could shed his sense of comedy. He had not the force of Hogarth, nor his weight of composing. His characters interpret themselves and are not presented to us in the jargon of a character part. They have, therefore, their own importance, and none other. They develop their own personality; but it cannot be seen if they are tasteful, or distasteful, to their creator. He paints them in their average of life, in the ambience of their ordinary surroundings. That is the gamut of Zoffany; and he seldom transcended it, or fell below its limits.

48

John Zoffany

50. A FAMILY PARTY: THE MINUET

Corporation Gallery, Glasgow

John Zoffany

51. ZOFFANY AND HIS FAMILY

Mrs. O. Benwell

52. SIR JOSHUA VANNECK AND HIS FAMILY

Arthur Devis

CHAPTER IV

ARTHUR DEVIS

OF all the painters who are included in our subject Devis is that one of whom it would be most easy to alter the public opinion by means of holding an exhibition. The prices obtained by his works, when they come from time to time into the sale room, are the gauge of this slowly increasing estimation in which he must be held. An exhibition, even upon a modest scale, devoted to his works alone, would reveal an English painter whom it is safe to compare with Longhi, and who deserves just that degree of fame and reputation.

Arthur Devis is one of the primitives of the English school. He was born at Preston, in Lancashire, as early as 1711. The facts of his life are still hidden in obscurity, and even the dates of his paintings are difficult to ascertain. He was never a member of the Royal Academy; while the lists of pictures that he sent to the Free Society of Artists are so briefly cata-logued, as a Portrait, a Lady, and so forth, that their identity is next to impossible to establish. It is to be noted that Devis did not join even the Free Society of Artists until 1762, when he was more than fifty years of age, so that it is to be concluded that the early part of his life may have been spent in journeying from one country house to another in pursuit of his profession. One thing, at least, is known of his early career, that he was the pupil of Pieter Tillemans, a painter from Antwerp, resident in London, who painted stiff interiors and neat, rather wooden figures, out of which the derivation of Devis is apparent. But the amateur must be upon his guard where this question of woodenness is concerned, for it is now the tendency to attribute any and every stiff little picture of this period to Devis. In reality, the difference is easily to be distinguished; for such is the mannerism, or natural technique, of Devis, and he was far from being either naïf or incompetent. Any genuine picture by him, which has been newly cleaned, is always a revelation of fresh, unconventional colour and the drawing is emphatic and decided. Devis knew exactly what he was doing. His effects are intentional, and not the result of accident or insufficient skill.

Even the genuine pictures by Devis are so numerous in quantity that it becomes difficult to make a choice of them for illustration. He is, too, more varied in mood than might be supposed. This is seen to advantage at Uppark, in Sussex, where a group of some twelve of his small paintings hang together on the wall of the staircase. They invite immediate comparison with Pietro Longhi, for this is the way Longhi is hung in Venice, in, for instance, the Palazzo Donà dalle Rose. The figures of Devis are brightly coloured cubes or cones. They make an impact upon their surroundings and are always a surprise. He is more fond of painting an outdoor scene than an interior. Longhi, by contrast, is a confirmed town dweller. Their technical accomplishment is about the same, with a slight predominance in favour of Devis, in spite of every advantage of training and environment in the case of Longhi. But his world was effete and petering out to decay, whereas Devis has something of the force and simplicity of a primitive painter.

We are enabled to illustrate several fine examples of Devis in which, perhaps, all his different phases and tendencies are revealed. He makes a bold use of the spaces between his figures, and it is this wide spacing, more than anything else, that makes him somewhat of a naïf or original. But his painting of landscape, and of dress and its accessories, does not give the least support to this contention, and his naïveté is contradicted by every-thing else but this special innocence or boldness. A conspicuous instance is his portrait group of the Till family (54). Mr. Stracey Till, in blue coat and breeches, is standing in the garden of his house by a low parapet, below which a river winds away into the distance. His son, Master John Till, a minnow or rather goldfish of a child, dressed in the elaborate coat and breeches of his period and holding a bow and arrows in his hands, is occupying not less than a third of the canvas to himself. Ten yards away, it cannot have been less, his mother sits on a garden seat with a plate of apples on her lap. His little sister offers one of these to her uncle, Mr. Edward Gilbert; while the other sister, who is a year or two older, kneels on the grass playing with a doll and looking up expectantly towards her father, whose gesture seems to indicate that she is favourite of the family. It is a curious fact about this picture that the wide intervals and freedom of the grouping give it realism and sincerity. The conventionality that is to be expected in minor pictures of the eighteenth century is opposed by this very woodenness that should have been to its detriment.

Another and most charming example of the same defect turned into advantage is the portrait of Mr. and Mrs. Richard Bull of Northcourt (58). Mr. Bull, whose family lived at Goldborough Hall in Yorkshire, was a Turkey merchant in the City of London, and it is probably in deference to this fact that, in the portrait, their feet are resting upon an elaborate and

53. AN INCIDENT IN THE GROUNDS OF RANELAGH

Arthur Devis

Lt.-Col. W. S. W. Parker-Jervis

Arthur Devis

54. THE TILL FAMILY

Sir Herbert Hughes-Stanton, R.A.

55. THE PUTNAM FAMILY

Attributed to Devis

By courtesy of the Knoedler Galleries

56. HORACE WALPOLE PRESENTING KITTY CLIVE WITH A PIECE OF HONEYSUCKLE
Arthur Devis   *Lady Margaret Douglas*

57. PORTRAIT OF A GENTLEMAN AND TWO LADIES
Arthur Devis   *Sir Herbert Hughes-Stanton, R.A.*

58.   MR. AND MRS. RICHARD BULL, OF NORTHCOURT

Arthur Devis

Jesse Isidor Strauss,

costly rug of that provenance. Both husband and wife are very young in this picture. They are sitting on chairs with beautifully worked backs on either side of a little round table of mahogany. The interior is wholly delightful. The chimney piece has an array of china upon it; a nodding mandarin in the middle, a pattern of vases big and small arranged to either side, and, at the two ends, a china bird of the Compagnie des Indes, we may presume. The rendering of these china objects, flecked and touched with light, has for accompaniment below it the silver basket of open filigree upon the table. Above the mantelpiece there is a landscape in a rococo frame and a pair of fine busts upon niches. Another landscape is framed above the door, while an enfilade of rooms lets in light through the high windows of the end. This may be described as one of the most rococo of interiors in English painting. The picture is signed and dated 1742. Mr. Richard Bull became, in later years, a friend of Horace Walpole; while the history of this picture is not complete if no mention is made of the fact that the family were kinsmen of Algernon Charles Swinburne and that the poet wrote much of his work at Northcourt. It would, perhaps, be fanciful to draw attention to the forehead of Mr. Richard Bull in this picture, for it invites comparison with the early portraits of the poet.

Another picture, which cannot be much later in date, and which is suggested for immediate mention because of its subject, is that which depicts Horace Walpole presenting the famous Kitty Clive with a piece of honey-suckle (56). There is no better Devis than this. The scene is a sylvan land-scape, with a far-off river and a pair of swans, the distance as it recedes becoming more and more shaded with groves. Horace Walpole stands by a garden chair of such peculiar design that its back, at first, seems like a crutch to support his arm. Kitty Clive, to whom he hands the sprig of honeysuckle, sits on a bench of that sort which is built round the trunk of a tree. Her wide brimmed hat lies by her side in suggestion of warm days and summer evenings. It was an impulsive gesture on the part of so calcu-lated a character as Horace Walpole; and, perhaps, this mood never befell him again until he was an old man and enjoyed the friendship of the Misses Berry.

A somewhat similar subject is the painting of 'An incident in the grounds of Ranelagh during a bal masqué' (53). The story of this picture is that two persons who were mutually attracted at this masquerade made the discovery, when the moment came to remove their masks, that they were husband and wife. They are standing in the picture by a stone sundial. His mask of a Turk or Hungarian, complete with the moustache of the Pandouk Hussar, lies on the stone, while he is still wearing the fur lined dolman or jacket of his disguise. His wife is more conventionally dressed, and her expression is, it may be, a little too serious for the romance of this adventure. Part of the delight of this painting is in the view of Ranelagh in the background. There is the Rotunda and a long row of arches or arcades, while a lake fills the foreground on the far side of which, walking on the grass, there can be dimly seen a harlequin, his bat under his arm, his hat upon his head, like a new kind of statue or garden term to be reflected in the water.

Two more groups by Devis of, perhaps, middling or intermediate merit are that of the Sefton family (59), a father and more substantial mother with their three sons, and the unidentified group of a man and two women sitting at a table under a tree (57). Here, again, the garden chairs are very conspicuous for their quaintness of design. The man has a long telescope in his hand, while the women are looking at a plan which seems to depict some bastion or fortification. The river, with a boat or shallop flying the flag, flows below; and, on the far side, there is a large mansion which has much resemblance to Syon House. No less than five dogs of different breeds, and including a Dalmatian, fill the foreground and must have made approach to this unknown trio of persons a risk not lightly undertaken.

The Putnam family (55) is a different kind of Devis. The old father and mother are seated in the open air at the edge of a colonnade or open room. There is pillared architecture in the painting, that is to say, though part of the composition is out of doors. The reason for this is because a large vessel in full sail and flying the Union Jack is floating in the bay, below the balustrade. Not only this, but the vessel is firing a salute and the old gentleman has his hand on a globe of the world, as though pointing to some particular spot in which he made his fame. His wife, who wears the black ribbed bodice which is familiar in many of Hogarth's pictures, has a wreath of flowers upon her lap, and this motive is continued in the two daughters, dressed alike and of the same height, who carry a long rope or wreath of flowers between them. They are standing in the shelter of this pillared colonnade or orangery, below a coat of arms upon the outmost pilaster, while one of the daughters who holds the end of that chain of flowers has a parrot perched upon her free hand. The rest of the composition is occupied by another sister who plays a harpsichord in happy disregard of the salute or salvo from the ship, and a young man, a brother or a cousin, who stands behind her and is given so little a share in the proceedings that it is a wonder he is included in the picture at all.

Perhaps all the qualities of Devis are shown at their best in the painting of Sir Joshua Vanneck and his family (52). There are no less than ten persons in this picture and their deployment into composition is a triumph of invention and arrangement. The characters are a mother and father, two elder sons, three elder daughters, and two little children.[1] Devis has solved the problem by taking them out of doors to the side of the river. The father and mother are shown, soberly and respectably, in a corner of the picture. Lady Vanneck sits on a wide garden bench, long enough for one of the eldest and one of the youngest of her sons to have their share of its comfort. Another and similar bench closes, so to speak, the composition upon the other side, so that the family are fenced in and enclosed as by a fence of hurdles. The river, as nearly ever, flows across the background with a wooden bridge alive with passengers and coaches. For this reason, no less than two of the usual telescopes are to be seen, and one daughter, who is remarkably pretty, has her glass mounted on its tripod on a stand, while another sister points at the river and the wide hoop of her pannier, her bodice and sleeves, and the prim gloves held in her hand, are given in delightful rendering by the painter. Yet another sister, for three of them are near together in age and allied in good·looks, sits on a chair talking to the brother who closes the composition upon the garden bench. It is only to be added that the foreground has an enchanting group of a young girl sitting upon the grass. She wears a dress of brocade and holds a basket of flowers, and her diminutive brother, another minnow or goldfish of a child, sits at her feet. Casting our eyes once more upon this picture we can see a church tower in the trees, a bowling green with its wooden pavilion, and another summer house painted gaily and giving on to the river.

It is, at least, probable that the Vanneck family is one of the most successful of the portrait groups by Devis. But its summing up of his curious contradictions calls for immediate assessment of his talent. Devis had a boldness which did not allow him to be frightened of anything that was required of him in painting. He would approach any and every problem in his own way, undeterred by difficulties. It is this personality in his method which is his quality. Devis is never, it is to be remarked, an aristocratic painter. His subjects have no breeding, for their personality, however accurate his presentation, is always imbued by the stresses of this person who gave them birth. His hardworking and conscientious hand was their master and never their slave. His pictures are not to be considered as 'so and so painted by Devis,' but always as a Devis, the subject happening to be such and such a family. At the same time it would be wrong to consider Devis as a mannerist, for his peculiarities do not derive from affectation but

[1] Horace Walpole is said to be the young man standing at the extreme right of this picture.

are rooted in his person and are a necessary part of his process of creation. Like a pianist who sits somewhat awkwardly before the keyboard, his stiffness of attitude is condoned as soon as he begins to play. It is only, thus, that his hands find their best action; and, in the same way, these tricks of woodenness find their excuse in the triumphing over difficulty which makes the beauty and the skill of Devis.

He occupies, it may be truly said, a place to himself in the art of the Conversation Piece. Behind his apparent formality there is hidden not much less than the competence of Zoffany. He has never the freedom, nor the serious solidity, the Handelian touch, of Hogarth; nor, need it be said, could it be expected of Devis that he should be a painter of the genius of Gainsborough. He is, instead, the perfect small master of the school. That this opinion of him is correct finds confirmation in the steadily increasing admiration to which he is treated. A painting by Devis, with his odd mannerisms, his woodenness, his wide spacing, his 'fish in a tank' stillness, is as much a work of art as a gouache by Lavreince or Baudouin, a drawing by Moreau le Jeune, or one of the little oils by Boilly fils or Schall. At the same time it is not with these names that he should be compared. His affinity, if it is to find an un-English equivalent, is to Pietro Longhi.

When that delightful painter of the Venetian settecento is invoked there are certain obvious disparities between them. For Longhi is confined in excellence to his interior scenes. He was the Venetian of the back canals, of the 'piccoli canali,' with their mouldering palaces lit with sconces and their brocade-hung rooms. That was his world; and when he ventured outside it, as in some curious sporting pictures in the Palazzo Donà dalle Rose, the results are to his detriment. But Devis, as we have seen, was as successful in interior as in outdoor painting. He was frightened of nothing and his interest never failed. His scope, therefore, is vastly larger than that of Longhi. Also, he could deal satisfactorily with much more complicated problems than those to which Longhi applied his talents. Two or three figures, at the most, make the epitome of Longhi. There is no instance in which he made a successful manipulation of eight or ten figures, all represented in portraiture, and in a landscape. No painting by Longhi can be compared to the Vanneck family by Devis. The scope of the Englishman is vastly larger than that of the Venetian. Devis is, in fact, a perfect instance of the little master; but it is to be doubted whether his excellence is known to more than a handful of people outside of English speaking countries. It is, therefore, Devis, more than any other painter of the Conversation Piece, who may be said to have a future.

Arthur Devis

59.   THE SEFTON FAMILY

By courtesy of the Knoedler Galleries

George Stubbs

60. COLONEL POCKLINGTON AND HIS SISTERS

Mrs. Charles Carstairs

CHAPTER V

GEORGE STUBBS

THERE is an aspect of eighteenth-century England which relates it to that other group of islands lying off the far shores of the world. England, like Japan, has resisted for nearly a thousand years. Their prosperity and seclusion led them to the breeding of certain fixed types. In Japan, the same school of artists, or actors, or sword makers, continued from father to son, down the centuries. In many families of the Court nobility certain accomplishments were hereditary; calligraphy, floral arrangement, football, poetry, swordmaking, heraldry, wrestling, and divination. These facts could be supplemented by their skill in the breeding of flowers and fruit trees and the nanization of the giants of the forest into creeping dwarves.

The parallel to England lies in the specialization of certain types. The pugilist, the gamebird, the racehorse, the foxhound, the bulldog, the prize heifer, the jockey, the hunt servant, such are the species that occur most easily to the mind. In every instance their connection is with sport, and Englishmen in every rank of life devoted themselves to their chosen pursuits with all the tenacity and devotion of the Japanese. A school of artists came into being who were concerned exclusively with various sports. Painters like James Pollard of the coaching scenes, like Alken or the splendid Wolstenholme, like Ferneley or Ben Marshall, developed talents which, because they were only bent to this one end, have been obscured and allowed to fall into neglect. Because the same audience still persists, these pictures or prints have kept their value in terms of money but are scarcely yet recognized as works of art. Nor, in the first place, were they meant as such. Alken and Wolstenholme, in their own minds, were sportsmen before they were painters.

Of all these men, descending from Wootton to Sir Francis Grant, the one great name is Stubbs. His lifelong occupation lay in equine painting, and in inspiration he painted a horse, at times, as if it was the Venus or Minotaur of his mind. This exclusive direction of his talent has kept him in obscurity, out of the knowledge of the world, so that it is only in very recent years that he has come into universal recognition as a painter. Only a short time ago, no authorities on the continent of Europe knew more than his name. None of them were curious as to his pictures. This was because

55

Stubbs was lost in a maze of sporting pictures and because every one of his paintings was hidden in some inaccessible country house. If he is, now, recognized as a painter of the importance of Zoffany, or, shall we say, of Longhi or of Guardi, it is on account of his Conversation Pieces. For, in recent years, he has become an established figure in European painting, and the few portrait groups for which he was responsible make it possible to mention him with Gainsborough or with Reynolds. There are some, indeed, for whom Stubbs is the favourite painter of the English eighteenth century.

George Stubbs was born at Liverpool in 1724. He is, equally with Devis, one of the primitives of English painting. At Liverpool he remained until he was twenty years of age: and, when he left that city, he lived at Wigan, at Leeds and at York. Even in his youth his passion for anatomy asserted itself, so that, as early as 1746, he is to be found lecturing on that subject at York Hospital. He, next, devoted his energies to making illustrations for a book on midwifery, published by Dr. John Burton, in 1751. Three years later Stubbs proceeded, by sea, to Italy, putting in at Morocco or Tangiers upon the way. It is known that he reached Rome, from which city it is recorded of him that he recommended the study of nature more than that of old masters. He had, then, at any rate the advantage, not to be expected in a painter of so insular a reputation, of having travelled to Italy. He may have remained abroad for a year, or more. Shortly after his return he began his work upon the anatomy of horses. This was to make his reputation, and he devoted all his energies to the preliminary studies. It was a process fraught with horror for squeamish stomachs, since it entailed the dissection of horses, and this was only possible in an environment where no one would object. He retired for this purpose to a lonely farmhouse near Horkstow, in Lincolnshire. Here, in the necessary seclusion, he worked for eighteen months.

Many years later, in old age, he described the process of these horrible studies. A bar of iron was fixed in the ceiling of his room, suspended by a 'teagle,' and hooks of various sizes and lengths were attached to it; under this bar swung a plank, about eighteen inches wide, upon which the feet of a dead horse could rest. To suspend a horse from the bars Stubbs passed hooks between the ribs and under the backbone on the horse's off-side. When studying movement he placed the horse's legs and muscles in different attitudes. His only companion during this gruesome labour was a Miss Mary Spencer, who became the mother of his natural son, George Townly Stubbs, and was so little perturbed by the odour of putrefying flesh that she lived in the painter's household for some fifty years.

It is even hinted of Stubbs that it was not only horses that he dissected.

Writing in the Sporting Magazine for 1808, after the death of the painter, an anonymous person, who knew him, says that 'a hundred times he ran into such adventures, at night, as might subject anyone with less honourable motives to the greatest severity of the law.' In other words, he was a bodysnatcher, if we are to believe this statement. The lonely farmhouse near Horkstow, will have gained, at least, an unenviable reputation. Giant carcases hung, by pulleys, from the rafters. The skinned bodies, like the statue of Moloch with open belly, would be large enough to hold the body of a man. It would seem, indeed, to have been a kind of Mithras worship upon which the painter was employed. The clanking of chains and grating of bones were its rites. That putrefying statue upon the altar sagged in its chains and thongs, and still had the articulation of its limbs. It cantered, or galloped, in ghastly parody of life, like a ghost from the bullring or the knacker's yard. Little by little, out of this sordid shame, the painter accomplished the anatomy and drew his task. But, when the drawings were completed, the difficulty of publication ensued. Stubbs could not prevail upon any of the engravers of the time to undertake this work. He had to learn the process himself, so that his book upon the anatomy of horses was not finished until seven years later, in 1768.

The fame of the painter was now assured, when he had already passed his fortieth year. The scientific accuracy of his horse painting, due to his intensive studies, gave him an advantage over his rivals. He began, from about this period, to enlarge his activity into other spheres of painting. It is from now onwards that his Conversation Pieces make their appearance. Most of them, in fact, date from the years between 1770 and 1795. But already he had preluded this advance by carrying his own art to the highest point that it has ever reached.

This might be termed his Yorkshire period. It is made memorable, above all, by the really extraordinary paintings belonging to Lord Fitzwilliam, at Wentworth Woodhouse. Of their value, to those who have knowledge of horses, the writer of these pages is not competent to speak. It is outside his province; but he can, at least, indicate their importance as works of art. It may even be that there is nothing in English painting to compare with them. The great and towering Whistlejacket is a horse that is worthy of Velasquez. This painting dates from about 1760. Whistlejacket was a yellow sorrel stallion with a white mane and tail. The original intention was to paint a portrait of George III riding upon this horse, but it possessed a prodigious temper and catching sight of the image of itself upon the canvas attacked it in a savage fury. Upon which the Marquess of Rockingham, the owner of Whistlejacket, decided that it should have a portrait to itself.

Stubbs, who was himself a man of gigantic strength, has put all his force into this painting of a stallion. It is a horse minotaur, the masculine deity of horses; and it would have required a Giulio Romano, a man accustomed to giants, to design the room which should be its setting. There are also, at Wentworth Woodhouse, a frieze of three horses with their groom; and, above all, the great frieze of brood mares, two foals and a filly. This must be the supreme horse painting of the world. The glossiness of their coats, the nubile softness and variety of their shape, defy description. The quality of this painting is perhaps best indicated if we say that Degas would have been without doubt its humble admirer. It has a bare, greenish background; and the absence of any landscape painted up to their bodies makes it like an Elysian field in which they are paddocked. Such is this painting, which is too great and primal in scale for the classical hall of marble where it is placed.

Another splendid picture of the same period is the Grosvenor Stag Hunt belonging to the Duke of Westminster. It was painted in 1762. The family, the huntsmen in their green liveries and the pack of hounds are shown, near the shade of an oak tree, in a plain that rises in the distance to the red rock of Beeston. The horses and hounds are inimitable; but this painter of animals has achieved, in this picture, a landscape that has the strength and solidity of Crome. It is a landscape of the Norwich school painted fifty years out of its time, for the flat plain of Cheshire is not unlike the plain of Norfolk. In addition to every other interest of landscape, and the painting of animals and foliage, this picture gains much from the splendid green liveries of the hunt. The figures, it would be not untrue to say, are as alive as in a painting by Canaletto. Another picture of brood mares and foals, belonging to the same owner, is also a splendid example of this painter at his most congenial work.

At about this time, also, Stubbs was engaged upon pictures of shooting. A set of four of these were engraved by Woollet; but they must yield, as works of art, to the painting in the collection of the Duke of Richmond, at Goodwood, of Lord Holland and Lord Albemarle partridge shooting in the fields. There are three horses in the picture, one of them held by a negro servant, and the action of the retrievers is of an almost extravagant accuracy. This picture is like a Wootton, painted by a master hand.

Two paintings at Welbeck, belonging to the Duke of Portland, may be the earliest of his Conversation Pieces. But, where Stubbs is concerned, it is difficult to know what paintings should, or should not be, included in this category. If these two pictures were by Zoffany they would be Conversation Pieces. But they are by Stubbs, and if they are included, then the

61. THE THIRD DUKE OF PORTLAND ON A WHITE HORSE

George Stubbs   *The Duke of Portland*

62.   THE THIRD DUKE OF PORTLAND AND HIS BROTHER, LORD EDWARD BENTINCK

George Stubbs   *The Duke of Portland*

George Stubbs

63. THE MELBOURNE AND MILBANKE FAMILIES

Lady Desborough

Grosvenor Stag Hunt, also, comes under this heading. These two paintings at Welbeck, which are small in size, show the Duke of Portland, in one picture with his brother Lord Edward Bentinck, riding or examining their favourite horses (61, 62). They are small intimate studies in which animal painting, portraiture, architecture, costume, are blended together into the perfection of a Dutch master. The scene is realized in exact atmospheric clearness so that it is, in both cases, neither a portrait, nor a horse painting, but a true and independent creation. These pictures have the mastery of Dutch paintings, though this is only said in comparison, for there is nothing Dutch nor Flemish in their execution. But they are paintings; and they could be looked at in any company of pictures, dismissing all other sporting subjects into the minor category to which they belong.

The group which involves direct comparison with this is the painting, of 1770, belonging to Lady Desborough. It consists of the Melbourne and Milbanke families (63), and may be the most familiar of all the Conversation Pieces of Stubbs. The shade of an old gnarled tree is thrown across the canvas, and drawn up in the shadow is a pony chaise, in which Lady Melbourne is sitting in a rose coloured silk skirt, with a white wrap round her shoulders. Sir Ralph Milbanke, her father, stands beside her. The grey, rough coated pony is splendidly foreshortened; while, in the other half of the picture, Mr. John Milbanke stands with his hand upon the neck of his horse, which is quietly grazing, and Lord Melbourne in dark blue coat with gold buttons, buff waistcoat and goldlaced tricorne, is astride a splendid chestnut. The distance is suggestive of rocky crags, and a lake, or plain, hidden in mist. If this picture is compared with the group of the Drummond family by Zoffany, to which it has many points of resemblance, it is the triumph of Stubbs over that essential painter of the Conversation Piece. It is not only the masterly painting of the horses, but the pink skirt of Lady Milbanke and the long lavender blue coat of her brother, Mr. John Milbanke, make this picture into a delight for the eyes. And yet, if it has a fault, it is that the grouping is a little too much posed and too obvious. This painting has not the naturalness and truth of those two pictures at Welbeck.

Another painting, of Colonel Pocklington with two ladies who are feeding his horse with flowers, is larger in size than the foregoing (60), but is like the half of that composition built up into a separate picture. It is, indeed, the identical tree that shadows them, but there is some difference in the background. This becomes, in fact, the type of outdoor portrait group by Stubbs, and there are other paintings by him which nearly reproduce this arrangement with only a necessary differentiation in the poses. It is a pattern which tends into monotony.

The picture in the National Gallery of a lady and gentleman in a phaeton drawn by two black horses (65) is signed and dated 1787. The painter was, then, over sixty years of age and it represents him in his mature powers. The horse and phaeton are superb; the lady and gentleman are full of character, but the landscape background is woolly and unconvincing. Yet, in all that great room in which this picture hangs, it most draws the attention. A great deal more success as a painting is achieved by his group of the Wedgwood family, dating from about 1780, and belonging to Mrs. Cecil Wedgwood (64). Mr. and Mrs. Josiah Wedgwood are sitting together on a white bench built round a tree. A specimen of his black basalt ware stands on a table at his side. Four children on horses or ponies are grouped, in most natural manner, close to them, while a little girl pulls two more children in a miniature chaise or phaeton towards them. This picture could be described as eminently sensible and portrays for us the plain and intelligent Quaker virtues.

In the multitudinous horse portraits for which Stubbs was commissioned all through his long life there is an increasing monotony, and the same consistent and reliable execution. But this receives a curious contradiction in two paintings belonging to H.M. the King. One of them represents an officer of the 10th Light Dragoons on horseback, a trumpeter and two troopers. It is one of the most amusing military pictures ever painted. Stubbs seems to have resolved, in his own mind, that the more wooden and stiff their attitudes the more play could he give to the details of their uniforms. The trumpeter and the two troopers stand stiffly in line, one of them, it may be said, presenting arms and the other holding his musket in another position. They are, therefore, seen like soldiers in a pattern book. The trumpeter, in his bearskin, is very fat, and like a post upon which to display pipeclay and gold braid. But his face is full of character and closely observed. The officer on his horse is in arrested motion, like the trumpeter and the two troopers. The warm air waits, quivering, for the bugle.

The other picture, which is painted in identical manner, shows the Prince of Wales' phaeton and Thomas the State Coachman, a pair of black horses and a stable boy (66). It is a delightful conception. The two black horses with their docked tails and manes, as black as black, but with white hindfeet, are held by the portentous coachman, who wears the scarlet and gold of his livery. Their silver mounted harness is a delight to follow along the black velvet of their coats. Then there is the phaeton, a masterpiece of elegance from the days when coach building and painting were an English art. It is most intricate and spidery in design, finely gilt and shining black in its patent leather. A black and white furred dog, of peculiar breed,

George Stubbs

64. JOSIAH WEDGWOOD AND HIS FAMILY

Mrs. Cecil Wedgwood

65. PHAETON AND PAIR

George Stubbs

National Gallery, London

66. THE PRINCE OF WALES' PHAETON AND STATE COACHMEN

George Stubbs

Reproduced by gracious permission of H.M. The King

is jumping up at one of the horses; and the black and white fringing of its fur makes a contrast with the clipped, black smoothness of the horses and their silver harness. A handsome stableboy, very smart and with powdered hair, looks on at this and is about to attend to the phaeton.

This pair of pictures, wholly delightful in their wooden artificiality, in their parade stiffness, in their paint and pipeclay, occupy a place to themselves among the paintings by Stubbs. We are informed that they are two out of a set of some ten or a dozen pictures of similar subjects, painted for George IV, when Prince of Wales. They date from 1793, when the artist was nearly seventy years of age, and were hung at Carlton House before being taken to Windsor, where they are at present. They possess, it need scarcely be added, no value whatever as works of art. But their position is an anomaly in the output of a painter who produced the Grosvenor Stag Hunt and the friezes of Wentworth Woodhouse.

For some years before this Stubbs had been experimenting with painting upon china. This was, in every case, upon Wedgwood ware; and after two years of continual research into the question of colouring in vitreous paste he was able to paint his charming scenes of Haymaking and Haycarting, the Farmer's Wife and the Raven from Gay's Legend, and other pieces in the same vein of taste. He also produced some work in the accepted Wedgwood tradition, a plaque, for instance, of Phaeton and the Chariot of the Sun, and a series of some twenty little cameo medallions of horses, to be reproduced in different colours.

The scenes of Haymaking and Haycarting are interesting because they are in the style, or are, indeed, exact reproductions in little, of his late paintings of pastoral subjects. These are not landscapes, strictly speaking, and it is to be wished that they might have been included in this book as Conversation Pieces. They give the idyllic calm and richness of rural England during the late eighteenth century. This is to be seen even in the Wedgwood plaques that have been mentioned. The haycart is drawn by four splendid black percherons and the peasants with their pitchforks, the peasant girls in white aprons and black flopping hats, are loading the wain. His oil paintings have the steady light of that declining noon, the dying of old pastoral England, of the smocked farmers in their kneebreeches and beaver hats. It is inevitable that these pictures should recall the pastoral Brueghel, for they have the same carefulness of detail and a like insistence upon the richness of the golden harvest. The yokels are lost for ever in it and, like the peasants of Brueghel, would speak a dialect that we could not understand. The Haywain of Stubbs, if we apply this title to all his paintings in this manner, has not the sentimentality and looseness of handling that spoils George Morland. It is masculine and vigorous, like everything to which Stubbs set his hand.

It is to be seen, in reviewing his career as a whole, that this painter has been mulcted of his fame. He is known for his portraits of horses and allowed, in this respect, a little eminence over Ferneley, or Ben Marshall, or Herring. But his equine paintings at Wentworth Woodhouse, which are almost unknown to the public, are equal to the best things of their kind in Chinese painting. It has been said that Degas would have been their admirer, and this is not loose praise for they are possessed of the quality and swiftness of Degas. The pair of pictures at Welbeck belong, on the other hand, to eighteenth-century art. They occupy no important place in this, but their merit is assured. The Grosvenor Stag Hunt, as a picture, is certainly the great achievement of the English sporting school. It is a picture, where Herring or the Barrauds are illustrations of the scene. The Melbourne and Milbanke families, the group of Josiah Wedgwood and his children, are in no way inferior to the finest Zoffanys. Finally, in his pastoral paintings, Stubbs has portrayed something that is lacking in all other pictures of eighteenth-century England. They are not pastoral affectation, but the rural truth.

The painting of Conversation Pieces was only his occasional interest. But it is difficult, in thinking of those rare instances, not to become convinced that the technical equipment and the vision of Stubbs were more competent than the skill of any other painter of the school, saving Hogarth, who was its origin. Zoffany, as we have seen, devoted himself to nothing else but these pictures, theatrical or in real life. His paintings of skill, the Tribuna for instance, are trivial and laboured compared with the great Whistlejacket, or the frieze of mares and foals. Zoffany's painting of a room, hung with the masterpieces of the world and crowded with living men, is not a work of art when it is compared with a painting of horses in which there is not even a background. Zoffany has the skill of rendering, but not the genius of creating. Stubbs, in contrast to this, has a power to which all the cleverness of Zoffany can never attain. His is only the world of human beings; but that of Stubbs is nature herself. Stubbs entered the different phases of his paintings from outside and did not, like Zoffany, paint them from within.

CHAPTER VI

THOMAS GAINSBOROUGH

THE mention of Gainsborough's name is the tragedy of the Conversation Piece. This is because the one or two most beautiful paintings in all its history are from his hand. They are pure, lyrical creations, owing nothing to any other circumstance. It is not because of the interest of the persons represented, nor through cleverness of perspective, nor counterfeit of glass or silver, that these little pictures are in their vein of poetry. But they are fresh and spontaneous. Their technical handling takes no account of difficulties and, decidedly, has no delight in them. They are small canvases but not miniatures. They have been painted in a run of inspiration, rejoicing in a gift, just realized, and trying the wings of it, playing with its brilliance and speed.

Gainsborough was, before all things else, a landscape painter. His pictures of persons are never psychological portraits: they are the physical presentation, and the passage of colour in its effect upon his scheme or mood. He was content with the pleasant appearance and did not seek the truth beneath it. When money and career came to him he was content to forego all truth and everything but his pleasure in the painting. His incomparable touch made him the servant of his sitters. He was at their command, but found his contentment in the play and exaggeration of his pretending. His portraits are, indeed, extempore schemes suggested by a hint of colour or of attitude. There is nothing monumental in their composing, but his grace and incomparable fluidity carried the pictures to their end.

He loved landscape and would have liked to paint it. But this meant country seclusion; and, by one of those contradictions so common in human beings, Gainsborough would never escape from the town. He was like one of those travellers in the ideal who stay at home. Perhaps he cared for music and for conversation more than for early rising and cold nights. Once he came to live in a town, whether it was Bath or London, the landscape fades and is no more than a dream or a suggestion. He painted some landscapes; but they were hints or memories and there was never time for more.

His gift, in its freshness and spontaneity, dates from the beginning. It continued all through his life, but found no new resources. He was living on memory, and on the impromptu of the moment. This natural gift was something prodigious and that has never been matched, so far as our countrymen are concerned. With little labour it lasted him a lifetime, for his mature portraits can have made no strain upon his intellect. Everything that he learned had come to him in youth.

It is necessary, now, to give the facts of this. He was born in 1727 at Sudbury in Suffolk; and all of his pictures with which we are here concerned were painted before 1760, before, that is to say, he was more than thirty-three years old. After that date he removed to Bath as a portrait painter, and then to London. These pictures belong, therefore, to his Suffolk period, when he lived in Ipswich. This part of England, which is nearest to the Low Countries, has produced a great proportion of our painters. Constable and Crome may be mentioned in proof of this. In both these men there is the influence of Dutch painting. Cuyp and Ruysdael, Hobbema and Van Goyen could not fail to affect the painters who came after them in a country so short a distance away and which presented much of the same character. But there is in Gainsborough, by contrast, no trace whatever of this foundation.

It is Rubens, and not the Dutch painters, who influenced Gainsborough. In his early career, he cannot have seen many original paintings by Rubens. The rare landscapes of that master were his inspiration later in life; but the difference between Gainsborough and the other painters of the Suffolk or Norwich school lies in that absence of Dutch solemnity and heaviness. It is as though he was racially different from the Dutchmen, while Crome and Constable had an identity, physical and spiritual, with the painters of the flats and polders. The aesthetic descent of the young Gainsborough, by contrast to this, is in the second generation from Watteau. This is because of the lessons he received from Gravelot on his visit to London in 1741.

Gravelot had come to live in London in 1733. He had known Watteau, and helped to prepare his drawings for the engravers. His employment in London was to make book illustrations, and after his return to Paris, in 1754, he was to become one of the great book illustrators of the French eighteenth century. His plates to Corneille and to the Contes Moraux of Marmontel are the best of these works. Eisen and Moreau le Jeune are by comparison less pure in style and their drawings show the beginnings of classicism and the Empire. Gravelot is the pure rococo in all its grace and delicacy. For all that, his method of drawing was precise and meticulous. He drew from dolls or figurines that he dressed in the appropriate clothes and hung in the right attitudes from the ceiling. There are, nearly always, three figures in his plates, and once this secret of his system is known, it

Thomas Gainsborough

67.   HENEAGE LLOYD AND HIS SISTER

Fitzwilliam Museum, Cambridge

68. PORTRAIT OF A LADY AND GENTLEMAN

Thomas Gainsborough

The Dulwich Gallery

69. JOHN JOSHUA KIRBY AND SARAH BULL, HIS WIFE

Thomas Gainsborough

National Portrait Gallery, London

Thomas Gainsborough

70. MR. AND MRS. BROWN, OF TRENT HALL

Sir Philip Sassoon, Bart.

is to be seen at work in his drawings. His figures, for this reason, have a convention which is absent in Eisen or in Moreau le Jeune. And they are little and subhuman, in the category of Cruikshank.

This is the painter who gave lessons to Gainsborough, and who will have shown him prints after Watteau. The fashion plates of that master, more especially, may have had an effect upon the student drawings of Gainsborough. It was figure drawing, and not landscape, in which he was his own master, that Gainsborough was to learn from Gravelot. His derivation from Watteau is, therefore, direct and simple. It is unlikely that any actual oil paintings by Watteau were known, then, to Gainsborough, but Gravelot must have shown him prints and, particularly, the easily accessible fashion plates published in the lifetime of Watteau.

On his return home to Suffolk, Gainsborough put into practice the lessons that he had received from Gravelot and combined them with his own essays in landscape. The resultant paintings are his Conversation Pieces. They brought him in a few guineas; but, by the time he was famous, many of them had long been forgotten. More must have perished than are left to us now.

The Fitzwilliam Museum, Cambridge, has a painting, by Gainsborough, of Heneage Lloyd and his sister (67). They are at the foot of a flight of steps, by a rococo balustrade. Heneage Lloyd holds a bow and his sister holds the arrow. No painting of children, by any hand, is better than this. Their youth and freshness sparkle out of the picture, which, for the rest, is rather dull and contains trees of a conventional woolliness that would never be found in nature. The Dulwich Gallery has a picture of a lady and gentleman (68); while, in the National Portrait Gallery, the picture of John Joshua Kirby and his wife is so similar in treatment and subject that they scarcely call for separate criticism (69). Nor have the plain looks of this quartet of persons inspired him to his finest efforts. This is always true of Gainsborough. These are dull people, of no beauty or interest, and Gainsborough, who could never paint badly, has painted them accordingly.

A charming and typical painting is the Young Lady seated in a Landscape, which is in the collection of Sir Herbert Cook, at Richmond. The billowing blue lines of her hooped skirt make it appear as if she is standing. She has a long and delightful bodice, holds a book of poems in her hands and shows a small and elegant foot. The background has formal trees, the façade of a classical house, high up and as if raised upon a terrace, and a statue upon an immense pedestal at the foot of which there are fountains spouting into stone basins. The French sentiment of this little picture is at once apparent; but what is Gainsborough, and himself alone, is the blue of the young lady's dress. It is a marvel of lightness and grace. It is the first instance that we come across of that quality which is to be found in Gainsborough's early paintings and nowhere else.

Mr. and Mrs. Brown of Trent Hall (70), belonging to Sir Philip Sassoon, Bt., is a little picture which contradicts our statement as to the absence of Dutch influence in Gainsborough. But Mr. and Mrs. Brown lived at Tunstall, Suffolk, and the sandy, gorsy landscape could receive no other treatment. The antlered oak trees, and the old farm buildings on that sandy slope leading down to the pond, are not less Dutch in appearance. But Mr. and Mrs. Brown are dressed with an elegance which does something to relieve the monotony of that scene; while their daughter, Anna Maria Brown, plays with a spaniel and is too young to think of more than that.

A delightful painting in every way and, indeed, the most lovely but one of the Conversation Pieces of Gainsborough, is the portrait of himself and his wife (3). It belongs, also, to Sir Philip Sassoon. The date of it is about 1750, when the artist was twenty-three or-four years old. The husband and wife are sitting together on a grassy bank. He has white stockings, a dark blue coat, a vivid red waistcoat, and wears a tricorne which is laced with white or silver. One hand is on his hip, and the other holds a drawing. His spaniel is at his feet, drinking out of a pool. Their little daughter, Mary, is between them. Mrs. Gainsborough is most exquisite and young. She wears a wide, hooped skirt of indescribable blue, inset with a panel of white silk which runs down to her feet. High above this, the blue hoop billows out above her hips; and she wears a bodice or surcoat of thin black lace, rendered in wonderful delicacy, but without care of detail. Coming forth from this, her arms lie along her lap. One hand clasps the hand of her child, and the other holds a flower. The distance is wooded and indeterminate. It is a background of green boughs and leaves, tied down to no particular spot.

Here again, in the figure of Mrs. Gainsborough, the French influence is predominant, but it has become personal and the property of none but Gainsborough. It is a nervous, quick, sinewy painting, in keeping with the painter's own thin and intelligent features. He is a very young man, and has not the patience of one who will stay always in the country copying the trees and fields. He has a career before him. Both he and his wife are extremely goodlooking, and not of the country or bucolic type. There is a great deal of temperament, in fact, in both their portraits. But, over and over again, it is the painting of her blue dress that is the importance of this picture, for none but Gainsborough has ever managed the paint in quite this manner. It is so different from the way in which material is rendered in a Metsu or a Terburg. There it is the simulance or counterfeit of the silk or satin. Here it is a painting of a blue dress, and not an attempt to deceive the eye. Also, the composition is more hurried than in a Dutch master. Their poses are static, for all time, impounded in a matrix that will last for ever and not lose its colour. But, in Gainsborough, it is inspired and hurried, just as, in life, no one would remain sitting on that green bank for longer than a few moments, and would not come back to it, day after day, until the picture was completed. The intention of the painter was to give the picture of life and not its imitation.

And now we come to what we believe to be, by consent of many lovers of pictures, the most beautiful painting ever done by an Englishman. This is the portrait of Robert Andrews and his wife (71). It is pleasant, to begin with, that it should still belong to the family of its original owners. It is still in that Suffolk of which it is the immortal rendering. Gainsborough himself was born within a mile or two of this landscape which we see. The scene is Auberies, near Sudbury, which was his birthplace, and the date must be 1755, as near as may be.

It is August, or September: the corn is cut and Mr. and Mrs. Andrews are at the edge of it, in a green field. He has come out with his gun to look for a hare, or perhaps the partridges are already in the stubble. They are at the foot of a great, old tree. His gun, with an immensely long barrel, is under his arm and he wears white stockings, dark breeches and a coat of primrose buff. He has a three cornered hat with laced edges. His other arm is on the elbow of the bench, while a retriever looks up at him, waiting for the sport to begin. What is wonderful in his figure is the loose, flapping lapels of his coat, the wrinkles of his sleeves and waistcoat, his gloves creasing at his wrist, and the twisted bags of powder and shot that dangle from his pocket.

His wife sits stiffly beside him on a hard iron bench, or garden seat, which gives the period by its curves. Her expression is demure and vaguely disapproving and she is very young, probably not yet twenty. Her hands lie straight in front of her, upon her lap. She has the long, thin bodice and the wide panniered or hooped skirt that was the fashion. Out of this, her two feet rest one upon another on the grass. The billowing extent of this skirt or pannier is so charged with the light blue, that is its colour, that the sensation of it is indescribable in words. It would be wrong to say that this blue is charged with electricity; but it has the colour of blue spray on one day in ten years in the Baltic or Northern Seas. It is no blue of the Mediterranean. Perhaps it is the blue of a fresh water lake, where the ripples have slight blue crests and the light runs through the bulrushes out to the swan white calm. There they ride, and arch their necks and look into the depths; and blue light breaks back from them into the reeds. This is that blue, in synthesis, billowing upon the panniers and down their crumpled sides.

The landscape is harvest and high summer. Yellow green grass spurts or fleeces from their feet into the harvest edge. The corn is cut and tied into stooks, leaving the bare stubble and its wounded stalks cut to the quick. All the cornsheaves are bound as prisoners: not a cornstalk stands. There are oak trees at the far edge of this, and then the harvest becomes pasture, through a white barred gate. There is a field of sheep, their fleeces flashing white in the distance, more fields and wooded slopes, not tall enough for hills. On the left, there are high elms for owl and ringdove, and through the boughs a church tower, near enough to hear the bells. The sky has great chariots and bastions of cloud, so there is wind and a far-off lowing of the herds.

The landscape of England has never been painted as in this picture. And so close is its identity that it would be pleasant to walk in the fields, in September, and recognize the scene. This painting has a fourfold or quadruple point. It is the primrose buff shooting coat, the blue pannier, the yellow green grass and the golden straw of the cornstooks. On two occasions, six years ago, when this painting was put upon exhibition in Park Lane, the writer of these pages had the good fortune to come upon it suffused, of a sudden, with the afternoon sun shining in from the West, and from low down in the heavens, for it was April. This made of it such an intermingling of buff and straw, or yellow, and light green and blue that the impression of it is unforgettable. It becomes light blue and greenish golden yellow in the memory. The colour of her dress remains, and the grass and cornfield; and then his coat comes back with its miraculous untidiness and its appurtenances for shooting, the press of the iron bench upon the knoll of grass, the tied and bearded cornstooks, the white gate, the far-off pastures and the elms.

If, in aesthetic and in history, English painting is three pictures, this is one of them. Each of them must be an epoch. The Wilton diptych is another; and, for third, we choose 'Amy, or The Long Engagement,' by Arthur Hughes, a painting which expresses the whole English nineteenth century and the Victorian Age in all its virtues and its failings. Mr. and Mrs. Andrews are the century before that, in extenso. Gainsborough never again painted at this level. It is his masterpiece and has the sensibility of every great painting there has ever been. Never again is there nature in his portraits. They are artificiality and impromptu. He finishes the draperies

Thomas Gainsborough

71.   ROBERT ANDREWS AND HIS WIFE

James Ward

72.   THE HALL PLUMER FAMILY

out of his head and interposes branches and a convention of green leaves. They become the portrait of a face, and a scheme of colour worked into a composition. There are no more cornfields, no pastures and no yellow grass.

And, in this picture again, there is the lesson of Gravelot. It is the preciseness of Gravelot, and his placing of the figures. It would seem in vain to seek, in this, for the influence of Watteau. But about the figures, nevertheless, there is the touch of that master. It has been suggested that, at this time of his life, Gainsborough had not yet seen any oil paintings by Watteau. He was familiar, though, with the engravings after Watteau, and it might be said that the figures of Mr. and Mrs. Andrews are his colouring or orchestration of those originals in black and white. This theory is to be studied in the painting of that coat and waistcoat, and in the blue crinoline. But the cornfield breaks its harvest at their feet in a vigour that was not possible to Watteau.

For a comparison of other figures in a landscape it is necessary to go to Velasquez. This picture by Gainsborough invokes comparison with the three shooting portraits, in the Prado, of Philip IV, his brother Don Carlos, and his son Don Balthasar Carlos. In each case it is the portrait of a figure standing in a landscape, while the circumstances of this trio of pictures puts them into a category of detail with the painting that we are discussing. They have guns and dogs, and the landscape rolls away from them into the distance. But their dress is the sober black or brown of Spanish etiquette. These are historical portraits; but, even so, the psychological power of the painter makes a drama of their anaemic pallor, their flaxen hair and Hapsburg lips. The treeless plain of granite surrounds them, and, in the distance, over the leagues of Castile, the blue peaks of the Guadarrama strike a chill into the air. They are cold and masterly paintings, done in detachment. Gainsborough is warm and happy in his eclogue, his oaten pastoral. His handling of the scene is more quick and vital than that mournful plain. Those are formal portraits: this is the Conversation Piece. It is the tragedy of this incomparable painting that it is alone in its kind. Within a year or two, Gainsborough had become a portrait painter. Never again did he rival with this picture of his youth. He had left the country and gone to the town.

CHAPTER VII

OTHER PAINTERS OF THE EIGHTEENTH CENTURY

THIS chapter, which must be a miscellany of names, has to deal with works that illustrate many different phases of the Conversation Piece. There are pictures by unknown painters, and paintings which form the unique contribution of masters who never again made experiment in this branch of their art. It will, therefore, be not in the least surprising if some of the most enchanting achievements of the school have to find their places in this mixed gallery. Painters born in the seventeenth century, and some who died in the nineteenth, form the combined body of this matrix or main principle of the genre.

There are, first of all, three names that begin from the seventeenth century. Gawen Hamilton, Marcellus Laroon and J. F. Nollekens were all born in that earlier time, so that their works belong to the age of Hogarth. They are periwig pictures, and will have been cumbrous and old fashioned in the time of Zoffany. Of Gawen Hamilton, little or nothing is known. He may have belonged to that family of painters of the same name who worked in Austria. One of them painted insects and butterflies in minute excellence; and another was an equine painter by whom horses, Lippizaner or Spanish stallions, and equestrian portraits are to be seen in many old castles in Czechoslovakia. It is probable that, like Cameron, the architect of Catherine the Great, this family of Hamilton were Jacobites. In Gawen Hamilton this strain cannot have been so strong, for he worked in England. His pictures, indeed, are peculiarly English and could be mistaken very easily for works by Hogarth. In the Vertue MSS. he is mentioned by the jealous Vertue as a rival to Hogarth. All that is known of him, in fact, are some notes in this collection. Vertue, it would appear, was a small man himself, and he says proudly that 'the most elevated men in Art here, now, are the lowest of stature,' and gives a list of names among which occur 'Mr. Hogarth Painter' and 'Mr. Hamilton painter.' He adds: 'these Gent. are five foot men or less,' and that curious item of information, together with the fact that he came from the West of Scotland and that he died, aged forty, of a cold or fever caught in coming from a supper at a club of artists, is the sum of all the information upon this forgotten painter.

73. MR. AND MRS. BENNETT AND THEIR TWO DAUGHTERS

Francis Cotes

Sir Herbert Hughes-Stanton, R.A.

We illustrate a picture of a club of artists (75), dating from 1735, which shows the influence of Hogarth to marked degree. It is, at the same time, a little weaker in design, and the figures have not that degree of character which Hogarth would have given to them. As a painting it is delightful but, compared with Hogarth, a little undistinguished.

Another picture by Hamilton, to which the title is given of 'The Vicar of the parish at the house of the infant squire ' (82), shows us the interior of a panelled room with figures that may, or may not, be portraits. They are characterized to the extent of Pietro Longhi, or to the personalities of the Rake's Progress. On the other hand, the portrait group of the Earl of Strafford and his family (74) is conscientious portraiture. It seems probable that this is the masterpiece of Gawen Hamilton. As a painting it is, indeed, not inferior to the Cholmondeley family of Hogarth. The background is a high room of earlier date than the picture, with a fine staircase seen through an archway. Two servants are upon the stair; and the staircase wall is frescoed with a trophy of arms and, in the manner of Laguerre, with figures of Orientals looking down from a balustrade. Lord Strafford, elaborately dressed and wearing the garter, sits in a gilded chair and seems a superior being to his wife and family. This is 'a picture which would draw attention to itself in any gallery and is among the best minor works of the English eighteenth century.

We come, now, to Marcellus Laroon. His is a mysterious figure, of whom little has been written and much might be said. The son of 'Old' Laroon, he lived himself to be nearly a hundred years old. He fought in Marlborough's Wars, was an actor, a harlequin and a soldier of fortune. As a painter, he began and remained an amateur. But he was an amateur of the calibre of Constantin Guys. And his peculiar technique is as individual as that of the Frenchman to whom we have compared him. It is so easily to be recognized that the little mention there is ever made of him is impossible to understand.

Marcellus Laroon is the master of many small pictures which cannot, unfortunately, be classed as Conversation Pieces. They are stage scenes, or the procession of figures through a wooded landscape. But there are also works by his hand which could not fit with more convenience into our category. There is, for instance, the drawing in the Print Room at the British Museum of a concert at Montagu House (78). This reveals the peculiarities of his technique at a glance. It possesses those essential tricks of drawing that are his personal idiom. His touch reveals itself in every line and curve. These traits are, perhaps, most clearly present in the manner in which he has touched in the tassels and flounces of the window curtain.

To the amateur of Laroon this passage, alone, would be a clear indication of their authorship. If we, then, follow down the drawing of the violoncello, close at hand, it is Laroon again and none other; while a glance at the lady who seems to occupy the chief place in the design will give us Laroon at his inimitable best. After this, the figure of the famous Heidegger seated, spectacles on nose, at the harpsichord, and wearing a tremendous and pedantic wig, becomes one of the typical and characteristic delights to be drawn from this peculiar temperament. The shoes of the pedant, seen under the harpsichord, betray that handwriting for which we are searching; while the other 'cello, played close at hand, and yet another lying ready propped upon a stool in the foreground, are the veritable Captain Laroon in every touch and stroke of the pencil.

More characteristic still are his small and thinly painted oils done, as it were, in a predominance of sepia and of olive green and possessed of an individuality all their own. Of these a good few come definitely within our range of choice, and there could be no better example than the musical party here illustrated (76). This little picture might be described as having the touch of Cruikshank in its crowd of figures. It is painted in semi-grotesque, as it were. The lightness and quickness are extraordinary. No fewer than twenty-six persons occupy the canvas; but there is no heaviness and no solidity. They are volatile and quickly moving. Mr. Ralph Edwards in his recent writings is certainly correct in supposing that no portraits are intended. It is a musical party: an ideal Conversation Piece, and the figures are no more drawn from actual life, however true their average, than the characters, say, from Cruikshank's 'Comic Almanack.'

This theory, it is true, receives curious and apt contradiction in the circumstances attending another painting by Laroon which we illustrate (79). It is a picture called 'A Musical Assembly,' of which Cruikshank made an etching for a sale catalogue published in 1819. There is an etched key by Cruikshank to the characters; the chief personage is termed Frederick, Prince of Wales, and Lord Pembroke, Lord Bute, Sir Robert Walpole, and others are said to be represented. But Mr. Ralph Edwards points out the unlikelihood of this. It is an imaginary Conversation Piece, and no more. This link, though, which connects Laroon and Cruikshank, is a delight to those who have the present writer's admiration for the latter of these artists. It is even apparent, we may think, that Cruikshank had seen other paintings or drawings by Laroon, and that his influence appears in many plates drawn by Cruikshank to illustrate the eighteenth-century scene.

The Duke of Buckingham's Levée (77) is another picture of the same tendency. It might represent the Duke of Marlborough, or the Duke of

74.   THE EARL OF STRAFFORD AND FAMILY

Gawen Hamilton

By courtesy of the Knoedler Galleries

75. A CLUB OF ARTISTS

Marcellus Laroon

76. A MUSICAL CONVERSATION

Sir Alec Martin

77. THE DUKE OF BUCKINGHAM'S LEVÉE

Marcellus Laroon

Samuel Howard Whitbread, E

78. A CONCERT AT MONTAGU HOUSE

arcellus Laroon

79.   A MUSICAL ASSEMBLY

Joseph Francis Nollekens

80.   THE MUSIC PARTY

Captain E. G. Spencer-Churchill

81. A GARDEN PARTY

Charles Philips

Tate Gallery, Lond

82. THE VICAR OF THE PARISH AT THE HOUSE OF THE INFANT SQUIRE

Gawen Hamilton

Sir Alec Martin

83. A MUSIC PARTY

Philip Mercier

National Portrait Gallery, London

84.   TWO GENTLEMEN TASTING WINE

Stephen Slaughter

Sir Alec Martin

85.   ALEXANDER POPE IN HIS VILLA AT TWICKENHAM

By courtesy of the Tooth Galleries

Joseph Highmore

86. THREE FIGURES IN A LANDSCAPE

Francis Hayman

Mrs. Derek Fitzgerald

87. SIR ROBERT WALPOLE AND FRANCIS HAYMAN

Francis Hayman

National Portrait Gallery, London

88.   A GROUP OF ENGLISH GENTLEMEN IN ROME

Thomas Patch

89. THE DUKE OF ROXBURGHE AND MISS MENDES

Mary, Countess of Ilchester

90. A GROUP IN FLORENCE

Artist Unknown

91.   CARICATURE GROUP OF IRISH GENTLEMEN

Lady Leslie

92. MR. WILLIAM ERNES OF BOWBRIDGE, AND HIS FRIEND, MR. TURNER
Joseph Wright of Derby   *Major V. H. Seymer*

93. GEORGE III AND THE DUKE OF YORK AS CHILDREN
Richard Wilson   *National Portrait Gallery, London*

94. HUGH, SECOND DUKE OF NORTHUMBERLAND, AND MR. LIPPYAT

Nathaniel Dance

The Duke of Northumberland

95.   QUEEN CHARLOTTE WITH THE PRINCESS ROYAL AND THE DUCHESS OF ANCASTER

Francis Cotes

The British Museum

96. THE DAUGHTERS OF THE EARL OF WALDEGRAVE, AND MISS KEPPEL

Paul Sandby

Victoria & Albert Museum, London

97. A FAMILY GROUP

Attributed to John Zoffany

T. E. Lowinsky, Esq.

98.   THE SITWELL FAMILY

J. S. Copley *Captain Osbert Sitwell*

99.   COLONEL EDMONSTOUN AND LORD ELIOCK

Alexander Nasmyth *The Marquess of Bute*

Chandos; any and every identity could be read into its personages. We must accept it as the levée of a nobleman; for, in truth, as we have said, it is an illustration of contemporary modes and manners. Perhaps, indeed, this picture verges a little too closely upon illustration. It has too many heads and shoulders in the background that only crowd the composition and add nothing to the picture. But so delightful a painter is Laroon that it is a pity to leave him. He has the strength of personality of a known person, and a manner and a technique that can never be mistaken.

A painter of at least one charming Conversation Piece is J. F. Nollekens, who was born in Antwerp and was father to the sculptor, Joseph Nollekens. He was known, therefore, as 'Old' Nollekens, and it is as 'Old' Nollekens that we think of him. His painting depicts a musical party outside Wanstead House (80), which was the home of Lord Tilney. It is, in fact, the exterior of that house which is not the least charming part of the picture. This solid Fleming had become influenced by Watteau, as can be seen by the figures in the background, which fact is confirmed in old dictionaries of painting in the statement that his subjects, like Watteau's, were often musical and fashionable conversations alfresco, but not imitations of that master. There should, therefore, be other pictures by Nollekens that await discovery. We illustrate here (26) a painting of rather earlier date, about 1720, of which the authorship is unknown. It can hardly be by Nollekens: it is unlike Gawen Hamilton: but we insert it in this context in order to show the excellence of its grouping and detail. The woman pouring out tea is admirably done, while the collection of china cups and saucers upon the tray and the case of bottles standing on the carpet derive from the Dutch or Flemish painters. Perhaps our illustration may help to identify some other picture by this hand.

Another attempt at a Conversation Piece, but one which is of an absorbing interest because of the person portrayed, is the painting, by Highmore, of Alexander Pope in his villa at Twickenham (85). There is no other portrait in which the poet is shown to us in the truth of his weakness and crippledom. This little puny individual gave to civilization The Rape of the Lock and The Dunciad. A servant breaks in on the stillness to hand him a letter; for this picture is, in truth, more a portrait than a Conversation Piece.

A word must be said, also, about Philips, a painter frequently to be met with and of occasional merit. A typical example is shown here; and many others, as good but no better, can be seen in country houses. If Philips is compared for a moment with Devis, or with Laroon, or even Nollekens, he sinks almost into insignificance. A painting of about his calibre, but interesting because of its scene and personages, is that of Frederick, Prince of Wales, and his sisters playing at their music in front of old Kew Palace (83). A picture of George III and his brother, as children, by Richard Wilson (93), is also included at this juncture, but needs no more mention. Nor is it possible for the present writer to simulate much interest in Hayman, by whom two sufficient examples are given (86, 87). It is probable that Hayman's best work was in book illustration, and in the decorations that he made for Vauxhall.

It is more profitable to turn to Pompeo Batoni. This artist was nearly the last Italian painter, and many Englishmen who went to Rome had their portraits taken by him (88). For some reason this is more particularly true of the Irish, and Ireland still contains many works by his hand. His contemporary fame caused him to influence English painters who visited Italy, as can be seen in the portrait group by Sir N. Dance, here given (94).

Not all English artists of Italian training show this derivation. It is not the case with Thomas Patch. This rare painter, who is unique in his works, was a native of Devon, born about 1720. He went at an early age to Italy, and continued to live in Florence for the rest of his life. By profession he was an engraver. His chief work in this direction was a series of prints from the frescoes of Masaccio and Filippino Lippi in the Brancacci Chapel. But, in respite from the labours of engraving, he was a caricaturist. It is in this connection that he painted some Conversation Pieces that are without equal in the art. They are interior scenes, in caricature, with portraits of the visiting Englishmen then in Florence. One of these belongs to the Duke of Roxburghe, and another is at Holland House. The Duke of Roxburghe of the time figures in both paintings, and the other portraits are of well-known connoisseurs and dilettanti of the day. In the former picture (89), the wall of the room has a painting of the Arno, the original of which picture is in the Holland House collection. In the other caricature by Patch there is a view of Florence out of a window in the room (90). He was, in fact, a skilled landscape painter. Another picture of the Arno, and a painting of the Piazza della Signoria, are at Holland House. This total of two caricature paintings, two views of Florence at Hampton Court, and two more of Florence and Venice at Holland House, is the sum of all that is left of Patch's peculiar talent.

It is known that he studied at an early age in Rome. While in that city he must have met the painter Pier Leone Ghezzi, one of the most gifted and individual caricaturists there has ever been. The style of Ghezzi is, beyond doubt, responsible for Patch. Ghezzi painted frescoes of comedy and carnival scenes in the Palazzo Falconieri at Frascati; while a numerous collection of his caricatures is in the Library at Valletta, in Malta, having formerly been purchased by one of the Knights of that Order. Ghezzi was a painter who, in one or two instances, achieved the transcendental. The present writer remembers seeing, in Rome, a painting of a carnival scene which was a prodigy of its kind and not to be described in words. Patch, though he never attained to the level of Ghezzi, is certainly unique as an English painter. It is to be imagined that he was an amusing companion, whose company was sought after by his countrymen. But, indeed, not even this is known of him with certainty. There is, however, always the possibility that other pictures by Patch may be discovered. In the meantime, his excessively rare works should be compared with the caricature groups by Sir Joshua Reynolds in the gallery at Dublin. There is some common denominator between them; but it cannot be said that Sir Joshua excels particularly in this genre and he attempted it on no more than four or five occasions.

It is one of the delights of the Conversation Piece that some of its major instances are the contribution of unknown names. There are pictures by artists who made their reputation in some other field. The charm of the unexpected must attach to these ramifications of the school, while the number of cases in which it occurs will show the innate talent of English painters in this type of composition. For the Conversation Piece is no isolated phenomenon. It is as frequent as the Dutch interior, or the Dutch still life, where, again, the proportion of unfamiliar names is part of the interest and attraction. Thomas Patch, as we have seen, is a painter of whom the known pictures could be numbered on the fingers of one hand. Alexander Nasmyth abandoned portrait painting after a few years and adopted landscape; while Copley was famous as a historical painter and only occasionally descended from that into the intimacies of portraiture.

John Singleton Copley is, also, an exception in another way. He was born in Boston, Massachusetts, when that city was still in English hands. He was English and Irish in origin, and the year of his birth was 1737. His early lessons came from his stepfather, who was a portrait painter, so that by the age of sixteen he was already accomplished in his art. It was only when he was thirty-seven years of age that Copley came to England, after having sent over a portrait to the Royal Academy which attracted attention. He arrived in London, in fact, in 1774; and, soon afterwards, undertook the journey to Parma and Rome in order to study painting. By the time he had definitely settled in London as a painter he was a middle-aged man. His historical paintings are not our present concern; but it may be said that the most famous of them are the Death of Chatham and the Death of Major Peirson. He was one of the first painters to insist upon historical accuracy of costume. His pictures were much admired: they were circulated everywhere in engraving, but they were, in fact, uninteresting Academical productions, in much the same style as his brother American, Benjamin West.

His Conversation Pieces, which are excessively rare, show him in different humour. Here he is the easy rival to Zoffany, and the mystery of why he so seldom practised this branch of painting is only to be explained on the assumption that, like Benjamin West, he made large sums from his historical pictures. Single portraits by Copley, generally of men, are not uncommon; but his groups are confined to two or three pictures and it is unlikely that any others will be found. The best known of them are the Sitwell family (98), and the group, in Buckingham Palace, of the children of George III (1).

The painting of the Sitwell family dates from 1787. Its commission is strange, considering the fame of Zoffany, unless Copley was a friend of the family. Nor is it possible to decide where it was painted; whether at Renishaw in Derbyshire, or in Audley Square. It is an interior in the Adam style, with a marble mantelpiece of that character, and the light flows into the room through a wide open window, with a view of distant hills, and through a window partly concealed upon the left hand side of the picture. Sir Sitwell Sitwell, Bt., about eighteen years old, stands in the centre of this room intervening in a quarrel between his two small brothers. Their sister, in a white dress and blue and white sash, sits in the window. The dispute is over a card house which Sir Sitwell is knocking over with his stick. One brother flies to him for protection, while the other holds up a hand of cards, one of the most brilliantly painted passages in the picture. The two little boys in their red and green suits are beautifully characterized. Their sister looks delicate and, indeed, a year later she was to marry Sir Charles Wake and die in childbirth. The light is wonderfully distilled throughout the room, and the painting is, perhaps, more solid everywhere than it would be in a Zoffany. A pot of geraniums in a corner of the room is, also, a trait which distinguishes the picture, for no instance can be recalled in which Zoffany ever painted flowers. This painting is certainly a beautiful thing. Long familiarity, since early childhood, has not dimmed it, where it still hangs in the Adam dining room, with red walls, that was its first home. In the year 1900, the late J. S. Sargent painted a portrait group based upon this composition and intended as a companion piece. It is, therefore, a conversation picture by Sargent, and, so far as is known, this is an unique instance in the output of that painter.

The other Copley, of which we give a beautiful illustration in colour,

John Downman

101.   THE LARKIN FAMILY

is the painting of the Princesses Mary, Sophia and Amelia, daughters of George III, from Buckingham Palace. This painting is of large dimensions. It is bigger in size than the Conversation Piece should be: but its subject and its beauty demand that it should be included. As a picture of children it is pure enchantment. The freshness and liveliness of the young princess at the left is more beautifully rendered than in any picture of children by Raeburn, while the baby princess in her wide feathered hat is not less pretty. Three spaniels play and sport in the foreground; while Windsor Castle, with its round tower not yet heightened by George IV, fills the distance. Is there any more charming painting of children than this? Their health and vitality overflow into this gay and cheerful design, up to the doves and clusters of grapes twined round the pillars and across the top of the picture. It is a curious fact, though, that this trellis of clusters and leaves is difficult to identify with the date at which this picture was painted. It has suggestions of Stothard, or Etty, in its imagery. This picture has every quality that should distinguish its English nationality and is, indeed, one of the masterpieces of the English school.

We come, now, to Alexander Nasmyth, who is well known in Scotland as a landscape painter, but who, in youth, was responsible for a few Conversation Pieces, of which the best is probably that of the Swinton family, of Kimmerghame in Berwickshire. This was painted at a time when two or three neighbouring country houses, Mellerstain, for example, had been rebuilt from plans by Robert Adam, and this picture reflects, therefore, a local or southern renaissance in the Border country. Captain Archibald Swinton and his wife are shown walking by the side of a stream. He wears a long buff coat and striped waistcoat and carries a book in his hand. His little son, in a red coat, stands by the side of his Shetland pony. The three little girls are feeding a pair of swans. The picture has, in fact, a marked resemblance to the painting, by Zoffany, of the Duke of Atholl and his family. This is, perhaps, more than a fortuitous similarity, for it is certain that Nasmyth had seen the picture. It has been impossible to obtain an illustration of this; but we give, instead, a group belonging to Lord Bute (99). This is an interior in the strict classical style of the new Edinburgh, with two old gentlemen talking together, and it may be taken to show the typical powers of Nasmyth, who later, as we have said, became exclusively a painter of landscape and did not die until as late a date as 1840, which gives a long pedigree from the ubiquitous influence of Hogarth, who is to be traced in this, as in every other, good interior painting of the Conversation Piece. The country houses of Scotland must contain many more paintings by his hand.

The picture that demands the next mention in this context is that which depicts the Tyrwhitt-Drake family in consultation over the plans of their house with, it has been suggested, the Adam brothers (103). The painter was J. H. Mortimer, a forgotten artist who deserves rescue from the oblivion into which he has fallen. There is, for instance, a fine portrait of Mrs. Chandos Pole at Radbourn Hall in Derbyshire which shows him as an excellent portrait painter. In the example that we illustrate it is, perhaps, the subject more than the actual painting that is remarkable. The Tyrwhitt-Drakes were in the process of rebuilding Shardeloes, their home in Buckinghamshire. If the figures on the right are indeed the Adam brothers the picture is unique, for there is no other portrait extant of all three of them. They had not long come down from Scotland. The expedition of Robert Adam to Spalato, in Dalmatia, had been undertaken only a very few years before, and this picture possibly shows them in their youth and at the beginning of their career. The aquiline type is very marked in two of the brothers, and is in exact accordance with what might be imagined of the architects of Kedleston or Sion. The porticos of Osterley, the fine moulded ceilings of 20 Portman Square, find confirmation, as it were, in those profiles of Greco Roman sensibility. It is pleasant to wonder if these are, in very truth, the designers of the Adam mantelpiece, the stair rails, the fanlights, the carpets, all the thousand details of the Adam style.

By Wright of Derby, the painter of The Orreries, we give a little picture of two men seated talking upon a wooded bank (92). It is a disappointment that no more than this can be said of a painter of his quality, but it is his nearest approach to the Conversation Piece. Our material, which verges at this point upon a miscellany, yields us, however, two paintings by Wheatley which throw a new light upon the artist known to everyone by The Cries of London. They are a pair of portraits of Mr. Ralph Winstanley Wood and his wife and children (107, 108). Among painters, Wheatley was one of the great names of the eighteenth century, and it is a delight to have these two Conversation Pieces by his hand. As a painter he is capable of many surprises. He was, for example, an excellent architectural draughtsman, as can be seen in some drawings made while he lived in Dublin. In this pair of pictures not only are the figures beautiful, but the background of ferns and trees is superbly done, as by a large and bold hand.

A drawing of the most ordinary kind, but first rate in execution, is shown in the plate after a drawing by Francis Cotes, R.A. (95). It is a Royal portrait. The subject is Queen Charlotte, the Princess Royal, and the Duchess of Ancaster in attendance upon them. Light washes of colour are all that the artist employs in order to give this impression of dignity. The

102.   MR. JAMES SETON OF TOUCH HOUSE, WITH AN INDIAN SERVANT

Philip Reinagle

Sir Herbert Hughes-Stanton, R.A.

J. F. Rigaud   104.   THE LOCKER FAMILY   By courtesy of A. de Casseres, Esq.

Julius Caesar Ibbetson

105. VIEW OF THE INTERIOR OF THE KEEP AT CARDIFF CASTLE

The Marquess of Bute

bright, thin blueness of the colour is applied most dexterously, where so serious an impression is intended from such slight means and such rapidity in drawing. Cotes, who was one of the foremost painters in pastel of the time, has achieved a wonderful solidity worked out of nothing. He is a minor artist; but so are Downman and Russell, two exquisite artists in little. It is the works of such men as these that raise the neglected Englishman, as artist, into a position where he can compete upon favourable terms with the contemporary Frenchmen or Italians of his time. A still more delightful example of Francis Cotes is his portrait group of Mr. and Mrs. Bennett and their two daughters (73). This is the property of Sir Herbert Hughes-Stanton, and we are enabled to give a reproduction in colour of this graceful and charming painting.

Philip Reinagle, who may be known to some from the plates that he drew for Dr. Thornton's *Temple of Flora*, that most lovely of botanical books, is shown here in his portrait of Mr. James Seton of Touch House, Stirling (102). This young man, excessively handsome, and in jockey cap and jockey breeches, is standing by his horse. There is an Indian servant close by, and his master is about to start off pigsticking, for the spear is in his hand. The National Gallery, at Dublin, has a group of Mrs. Congreve and her children which is a curious specimen of Reinagle. In style, it is like an over-emphasized Zoffany, conspicuously German, in fact, but loaded with pleasant detail, more especially in her absent husband's sword and cocked hat by a table in the corner. This picture, which is not reproduced here, should lead to the identification of more portrait groups to which the name of Zoffany is nearly, but not quite, applicable. By J. F. Rigaud, a Frenchman, who worked in London and painted altar pieces and ceilings which no one has cared to find, there is a family group which may serve to attract attention to another forgotten name (104). By Paul Sandby, the master of aquatint, we give a water colour drawing of the three daughters of Earl Waldegrave (96). There is a family group of an unknown hand and belonging, now, to Lady Hudson (25), which depicts a father and mother surrounded by no less than nine children. But the interest of this picture is in the background, where there is a formal garden of clipped yews and hornbeam which is nearly identical with the garden in a picture at Buckingham Palace attributed to de Hoogh. By Henry Edridge, a delightful portraitist in little, we give a drawing in pencil and water colour of a gentleman and two children (106). This belongs to the age of Ingres. By Downman we give the Larkin family (101), an ambitious group of a mother and eight children, and the oil painting, in the National Gallery, of Sir Ralph Abercromby in conversation with his secretary (100). Something in the attack of this little picture shows the unfamiliarity, and the consequent interest, of Downman in this medium in which he worked so seldom. The black suit of the secretary, his powdered hair and the sharp cut of his profile are a delightful passage from the hand of one of the most charming of all lesser masters of the British school.

Finally, there is an oil painting by the landscape artist, Julius Caesar Ibbetson, showing a large group of gentlemen deep in discussion among the ruins of an old castle (105). This picture is the property of Lord Bute, and the ruins in question may be those of Cardiff Castle. And, to end with, there are two equine subjects; a picture, by J. Ward, of the Hall Plumer family in the meadows in front of their house (72), and a painting, from Castle Howard, of the Earl of Carlisle and his family in Phoenix Park, Dublin (109). This is by Francis Wheatley, dating from the period when he made the architectural drawings of Dublin that have already been mentioned. The two ladies in their phaeton are as lovely as a plate from Heideloff's Gallery of Fashion, and the whole picture reveals Wheatley in one of those unknown phases of his talent that make of him so much more interesting an artist than the mere designer of The Cries of London.

106. A GENTLEMAN AND TWO CHILDREN

Henry Edridge

Victoria & Albert Museum, London

107. RALPH WINSTANLEY WOOD AND HIS SON, WILLIAM WARREN

Francis Wheatley

By courtesy of the Knoedler Galleries

108. MRS. RALPH WINSTANLEY WOOD AND HER TWO DAUGHTERS

Francis Wheatley

By courtesy of the Knoedler Galleries

Francis Wheatley

109.   THE EARL OF CARLISLE IN PHŒNIX PARK, DUBLIN

The Earl of Carlisle

J. M. W. Turner   110. A MUSICAL PARTY AT PETWORTH   *The Tate Gallery, London*

CHAPTER VIII

THE NINETEENTH-CENTURY CONVERSATION PIECE

FOR some years before the death of Zoffany in 1810 the Conversation Piece had been in decline. No groups by Zoffany himself can be dated with any certainty after the close of the century. During the long Napoleonic wars this style of painting languished and is only to be found reflected, perhaps, in some of the drawings by Rowlandson. It seems to have revived almost immediately upon the cessation of the war. In painting, in architecture and in literature the English were, then, the leading nation of the world. It is only necessary to mention Turner and Constable in landscape, Lawrence in portraiture; Sir John Soane, Nash and all the lesser architects of the Regency; Sir Walter Scott, Byron, Shelley, Keats. But the movement was clouded by adversity. Byron, Shelley and Keats died in their youth. So did Bonington, the most gifted of the painters.

But the Conversation Piece, which mirrors the calmer waters of life, pursued its not inconsiderable career. It echoes the rising prosperity of the age and comes to a stop in the very heart of Victorian materialism. This final period, which starts from 1815 and ends in 1860, contains many delightful things, but no famous names. There are, indeed, minor painters like A. F. Chalon who deserve, and may one day achieve, a more lasting fame. But, although so near to the Conversation Piece, we have searched his works in vain to find a picture which we could reproduce. The same stricture must be applied to J. F. Lewis, one of the most gifted painters of his time. He had every quality that goes to the making of a Conversation Piece, but never exercised those faculties, except upon Spanish or Oriental scenes. He must, therefore, be excluded.

Probably C. R. Leslie is the painter of the most important portrait group for the lapse of a generation after the death, or retirement, of Zoffany. Like Copley and like Benjamin West, Leslie was of American parentage, but he was born in London in 1794. As soon as the peace permitted, Leslie went abroad to study painting in Paris and in Belgium. Immediately on his return he began to exhibit at the Royal Academy and, much later in his life, became Professor of Painting there. He was summoned to Windsor, soon after her accession, to paint the portrait of Queen Victoria receiving the Sacrament at her Coronation. He is now known, if known at all, chiefly for his Memoirs of Constable, who was his friend. He died in London in 1859.

Leslie painted at least two Conversation Pieces, one of them, as we have said, being the most important picture of its kind since the eighteenth century. This is a group of the Grosvenor family, and hangs in Bourdon House, the Duke of Westminster's London home. It shows the interior of the old Grosvenor House with immense canvases by Rubens covering the walls. This picture was painted in 1833 and is a faithful copy of the fashions of that time, especially in the high waists and feathered hats that were worn then. The little children in the painting are particularly natural and delightful. This portrait group, painted only a century ago, has already the quality and patina of an old master. But in no way does it show influence from the eighteenth century. Zoffany might never have existed, so far as Leslie is concerned. Instead, it is marked with the study of Lawrence and of Van Dyck; while its setting is, of course, the gilded and opulent work of the late Regency. The grouping of so many figures and the general harmony of this interior deserve the highest praise.

The other picture by Leslie to which we referred is his painting of the library at Holland House (111). This is a smaller picture, and a less ambitious composition altogether, for it only contains four figures. But the painting is, so to speak, an invaluable document because of the interesting associations of the people concerned. There is no house of that time of which we would sooner have such a memorial, unless it be Gore House, nearby in Kensington, with Lady Blessington, Count d'Orsay and their motley company. In this picture, Lord and Lady Holland are seated in the library talking to their secretary, while the librarian takes down a book from the shelves and is in earnest conversation with the mistress of the house. The Jacobean interior is amazingly well painted, and down at the far end a young boy is to be seen poring over a bookcase. So accurate, indeed, is the representation of the mantelpiece and woodwork that the picture resembles one of the interiors of bygone times by Joseph Nash.

A large miniature, painted upon ivory, by Thorburn, is reproduced at this point of our context (117). It is a super-miniature, heroic in scale where miniatures are concerned, and attaining to the dimensions and importance of the Conversation Piece. But, still more, it is its subject which may interest us. This is the great Duke of Wellington with his grandchildren, one of whom was to succeed him as third Duke and to die as recently as within the last few months. As a picture it is, in fact, a link between the present and the past. The style is like a combination of C. R. Leslie and Augustus Egg, a painter who is due for immediate mention at our hands.

C. R. Leslie

111.   THE LIBRARY AT HOLLAND HOUSE

Earl Grey

112. SIR RERESBY SITWELL AND HIS BROTHER AND SISTERS

Octavius Oakley   *Captain Osbert Sitwell*

113.   THE WESTON FAMILY

Ben Marshall   *G. D. Widener, Esq.*

John Ferneley

114.   THE FERNELEY FAMILY

T. B. Yuille, Esq.

John Ferneley

115.   COUNT D'ORSAY AT HYDE PARK CORNER

By courtesy of the Tooth Galleries

John Ferneley

116. JOHN FERNELEY AND HIS DAUGHTER ON HORSEBACK

Contemporary with C. R. Leslie was the animal painter J. Ferneley. This painter who, with Ben Marshall, is beginning to emerge into the eminence that he deserves, has left us at least three pictures that we can reproduce. There is a group of himself and his family on horseback (114); and a picture, which is much more attractive, of himself and his daughter, again on horseback, but altogether subordinated in importance to a splendid hooded carriage, a chariot or a phaeton, which is waiting outside a building (116). It is drawn by a pair of horses. The postilion is mounted on the leader but the carriage still waits empty for its occupants to come out of the house. Near at hand, a horse held by a tophatted groom is, also, in waiting.

The third painting by Ferneley cannot, strictly speaking, be called a Conversation Piece, but its inclusion has been irresistible. It portrays Count d'Orsay riding his favourite hack in Hyde Park, by the Achilles statue (115). In the background there are the coaches and carriages of Park Lane, and a mounted Amazone galloping towards us with veil floating behind her from her tall hat. Count d'Orsay is dressed in the height of his dandyism; though, perhaps, the most delightful part of the whole painting is his cabriolet waiting for him, held by a little groom, or tiger. This picture, and the one that preceded it, give us that world of luxury and polish to which the young Disraeli aspired in his novels. Carriage building was one of the arts of London, a fact of which there should be evidence, next summer, when the last of the family coaches attend the Coronation. The cabriolet of Count d'Orsay is a miracle of elegance. It is the mythical elegance of the Englishman, borne out in the conspicuous neatness of its master. This is the English aristocrat and dandy as Baudelaire saw him. The early period of Constantin Guys, when he lived in London, is his attempt to capture this atmosphere, and we see it, too, in the fashion drawings by Numa whom Baudelaire admired and extolled.

After the lightness of Ferneley it is inevitable that Ben Marshall should seem heavy and unrefined. His portrait group of the Weston family (113) is conscientious and wooden. This is not the métier of Ben Marshall who, in his own sphere, is not easily approached. But, following closely upon Ferneley, there is Sir Francis Grant of whom the Melton Breakfast (126), which is too well known to require description, is the master work. This is a perfect example of the Conversation Piece. It has long been famous, but it is, as well, a work of art. A painting by Sir Francis Grant, which is not so well known, is his picture of Queen Victoria riding out from Windsor Castle (127). She has Lord Anglesey in attendance upon her and the 2nd Marquess Conyngham, son of the favourite of George IV. This was painted in 1839; and it is, perhaps, the last English picture, until modern times, which has direct quality and is neither comical nor curious.

Following upon these two conventional scenes a rare curiosity is reproduced, which has, indeed, never before been illustrated. It is a painting of a Musical Party at Petworth by J. M. W. Turner (110). This might be termed a transcendental experiment, for it reveals that tireless searcher in a mood which is without counterpart in his work. It is a piece of abstract impressionism and may remind us of the most recent experiments of Picasso. And yet, in some curious way, the time signature is upon it. It is Turner at work in the age of Sir Thomas Lawrence. The neck and shoulders of the young woman speak of Lawrence or of Wilkie. But no other painter of that day could dissolve his vision into this abstract informality. It is, and could only be, a Turner; even if it points forward a century or more into the future.

A Conversation Piece by Constable (118) has little but its curiosity to commend it, and the plate that follows by Margaret Carpenter (120) is more successful as a portrait group. A drawing by Poyntz Denning of the children of Elhanan Birknell (122) may have the unfamiliarity of its names as its chief attraction. It is a nice average of the water colour drawings of the time; but in no way to be compared with Oakley, the master of this style. A painting of the Heygate family by Ozias Humphry (119) is a fair example of its author. A more attractive picture is the poet, Samuel Rogers, with two young ladies (123), by Frank Stone, father of the once-beloved Mr. Marcus Stone, R.A. And it is clear from this that we are approaching the end.

Apart from C. R. Leslie and Sir Francis Grant, the Conversation Piece, at this time, resolves itself into isolated and individual delights. The picture is no longer a work of art but becomes a curiosity of detail or of contemporary life. We reproduce a portrait group by a forgotten painter, Partridge, which has the interest of having been composed as pendant to a picture by Copley (121). But there are minor artists, Oakley, for instance, who worked chiefly in Derby and the country houses in the neighbourhood, and who deserves the honour of a small exhibition to himself. He was the master of little conversations in pencil and water colour (112), paying particular attention to likeness and to niceties of dress. The writer, who has seen many of his drawings, can vouch for the hereditary truth of resemblance as shown in descendants of his subjects. There must be many more local artists of his eminence and character. Local centres like Norwich, Exeter or Newcastle are certain to have possessed his equivalent; and, then, there is Edinburgh, where more than one painter of his kind will have found a living. This is, in short, a branch of research in which any intelligent amateur can engage. The little portrait groups in pencil and water colour are an immense and

117. THE DUKE OF WELLINGTON WITH THE CHILDREN OF LORD CHARLES WELLESLEY AT STRATHFIELDSAYE

Robert Thorburn

Lord Gerald Wellesley

118.   ALEXANDER POPE AND HIS FAMILY

Ozias Humphry

119.   THE HEYGATE FAMILY

By courtesy of the Leger Gallerie

120.   THE HICKS CHILDREN

Margaret Carpenter

By courtesy of the Leger Galleries

John Partridge

121. SIR GEORGE SITWELL AND HIS FAMILY

Captain Osbert Sitw

unsurveyed field in which there are many surprises still lying hidden. It is the art of the family album; and, on occasion, it is members of the family who possessed the talent.

The next and final phase of the movement comes with the pre-Raphaelites. But even before the foundation of the actual brotherhood, there were painters with the same tendency to detail who were instinctive fore-runners of the reform, Augustus L. Egg for example. This oddly named individual, of whom we know that he was a good amateur actor and a friend of Dickens, may be seen by the curious upon the walls of the Tate Gallery. And he was a painter of decided talent. Above all, his pictures are the perfect period piece. The two first decades of Queen Victoria's reign are presented to us as under a glass case, a dome enclosing something that will never move. This is the far-out centre of the nineteenth century. Nothing has reached to it of the eighteenth century: and of the twentieth there is no hint or sign. There is hardly another painter, now, so uncared for and so undisturbed as Egg. He is a haven, or shall we say a middle class parlour, of peace and rest. It is probable that diligent search in provincial galleries, and in rich villas built between 1840 and 1860, would bring to light some more pictures by this painter of Canonbury and Islington.

We illustrate, at this point, a most extraordinary and unique picture by an unknown hand (125). It is the Victorian interior of 1830 to 1840 pre-sented to us as by the stereoscopic lens. As a painting of detail and per-spective this picture is a masterpiece in little. The harmony of that dim interior is wonderfully portrayed; while the objects upon the table and the mantelpiece are painted with all the skill of Zoffany. There is no conjecture as to the name of the painter, who may have been a woman, from the feminine feeling of this interior. It is the sherry hour. The girl with her back turned is handing sherry and a slice of cake to the old lady who is seated in the corner. The sherry tray rests upon a typical mahogany table of the period. There are wax flowers, under a glass shade, upon the table. The oil lamps are no less indicative of the time. All things are in harmony. It is such unknown paintings as this that are the delight of the English Conversation Piece.

There are other men of that generation, Maclise, Mulready or Dyce, by whom there may be Conversation Pieces in existence. And there is Frith, the painter of Derby Day and the Railway Station, who, it is certain, painted pictures of this kind.

Finally, there are the pre-Raphaelites. Not Rossetti, Burne-Jones and the mediaevalists: but the painters of contemporary life, Ford Madox Brown or Holman Hunt. But, unfortunately, the 'problem' occupied their minds. Every picture had to tell a story, or have a meaning, so that the Conversation Piece was hardly serious enough to occupy their unremitting attention. That well known painting, The Last of England, by Ford Madox Brown, would fall within our category were it not for the sentiment underlying its meticulous detail. The same strictures apply to so many pictures by Holman Hunt and J. E. Millais which come almost within our grasp, and then elude us by the twist of a symbol or by a hidden meaning. We illustrate, however, a picture by H. T. Wells which fulfils every requirement of its genre.

Lesser painters, working upon the pre-Raphaelite principles, are for ever hovering near to the borders of the Conversation Piece. 'Amy, or The Long Engagement,' that epitome of the mid-nineteenth century by Arthur Hughes, is the perfect example of this propinquity. A young curate and his betrothed are talking together in a spring wood. The name 'Amy' is carved upon the trunk of a tree; and the state of this inscription bordered with moss and lichen gives us to believe that their troth was plighted many years ago. Their marriage day is still distant. But meanwhile, all round them, nature is at work. The birds are building their nests, the trees burst into leaf; it is only themselves who are prevented and delayed. This is, as we have said before, perhaps the most typical picture of mid-Victorian England. It was painted by the last survivor of the pre-Raphaelite school, who died as recently as 1915. Other men who were affiliated at some time in their lives to its principles, Seddon, Windus, Martineau or Brett, painted interiors which are Conversation Pieces, all but for the 'problem.' The 'Last Day in the Old Home' by R. B. Martineau is a case in point. It should be added that in this sort of picture the pre-Raphaelites generally painted the portraits of their friends, probably because of the immense number of sittings that their method necessitated, so that such a painting as this is some particular friend of Martineau posing as the reprobate in the old home, and this picture relates itself, in a sense, more to the theatre scenes of Zoffany or de Wilde.

The appropriate end to these pages is in the drawing room of George du Maurier, who typifies for us the 'seventies and 'eighties of last century, with touches, even, of the rising aestheticism. There are, literally, hundreds of little Conversation Pieces by du Maurier, one for nearly every week's issue of *Punch*. They are clear instances of the drawing being done first and the text being added later. His play was round the same ever-recurring types; and, as often as not, the motto below the drawing adds nothing to what the artist has already told us. The prodigal plenty of the late Victorian era is proved in the careless and unnecessary scratches of du Maurier's pen,

122. THE CHILDREN OF ELHANAN BIRKNELL

S. P. Denning

Victoria & Albert Museum, London

123. SAMUEL ROGERS, THE HON. MRS. CAROLINE NORTON, AND MRS. PHIPPS

Frank Stone

National Portrait Gallery, London

W. and H. Barraud

124.   THE BEAUFORT HUNT LAWN MEET AT BADMINTON

The Hon. Mrs. Macdonald-Buchanan

125. A VICTORIAN INTERIOR

Artist Unknown

Oliver Brown, Esq.

Sir Francis Grant

126.   THE MELTON BREAKFAST

Lord Cromer

all of which had, afterwards, to be carefully reproduced by Swain or his assistants upon the woodblock.

It is a happy world. There are tea parties upon lawns; picnics upon the river; the curate comes to dinner; young ladies, in bustles, are playing tennis; Polish pianists give recitals in drawing rooms; the aesthetes air their views and annoy everyone; Mrs. Cimabue Brown and the Postlethwaites

A FELT WANT.

Eligible Young Aspirant. 'And do you really approve of Gymnastics for Young Ladies, Mrs. Prendergast?'

Proud Mother. 'I do, indeed, Mr. Mildmay, and always have. I can assure you that there is not one of my Daughters that couldn't knock down her own Father!'

From a *Punch* Cartoon by George du Maurier.

are ever arguing; drawing rooms have peacock fans and pieces of blue and white china; aesthetic women are dressed in sad seagreen.

But it was not all thus. A painting by Barker, our penultimate illustration, shows a shooting party at Sandringham in 1870 (129). The Prince of Wales holds the foreground, and round him are grouped his friends, Lord Chesterfield, Lord Londesborough, the Duke of Beaufort. This is the non-aesthetic England of the day. It cannot be called anti-aesthetic, because it is doubtful if it had ever heard of the aesthetics. Art had stopped short of such persons half a century before. Nor, if we look at these figures against their background of ferns and bracken, has there been much change, sartorially, since their day. Two of the sportsmen are wearing bowler hats; but, except for that, their clothes are nearly identical with those of today. They are in living memory; but this book draws to its conclusion with a portrait of a person still living in our midst. It is a painting, by Winter-halter (128), of the Duke of Wellington presenting a casket to Queen Victoria on 1st May 1850, the birthday of the Duke of Connaught, who is the little baby shown in the picture.

From Moses' *Modern Costume* (1823).

127. QUEEN VICTORIA RIDING OUT AT WINDSOR CASTLE

Sir Francis Grant

Reproduced by gracious permission of H.M. The King

128. THE DUKE OF WELLINGTON PRESENTING A CASKET ON PRINCE ARTHUR'S BIRTHDAY

F. X. Winterhalter

Reproduced by gracious permission of H.M. The King

129.   A SHOOTING PARTY AT SANDRINGHAM

J. J. Barker   *By courtesy of the Leger Galleries*

130.   A PORTRAIT GROUP

H. T. Wells   *Mrs. Street*

NOTES ON THE ILLUSTRATIONS

By MICHAEL SEVIER

COPLEY, JOHN SINGLETON, R.A.
(1737–1815)

1. THE CHILDREN OF GEORGE III.
    Oil, 104×61 inches.
The three Princesses are the three younger daughters of George III and Queen Charlotte. Princess Mary, afterwards Duchess of Gloucester, is on the left and the Princesses Sophia and Amelia are on the right.
Painted for George III at Windsor Castle.
Signed and dated: *J. S. Copley, R.A.*, 1785.
Coll.: *His Majesty the King, Buckingham Palace.*

HEIDELOFF, NIKOLAUS WILHELM
(Born 1761)

2. A COLOURED AQUATINT FROM *Gallery of Fashion.*
The *Gallery of Fashion* was a periodical issued by Heideloff in monthly parts from April 1794 to March 1803. The whole publication comprises 217 aquatint plates. The present example, entitled 'Morning Dress,' is taken from the January, 1799, issue.

GAINSBOROUGH, THOMAS, R.A.
(1727–1788)

3. THE ARTIST, HIS WIFE AND CHILD.
    Oil, 36×38 inches.
Gainsborough, his wife, Margaret Burr, whom he married in 1745, and their elder daughter Mary.
Painted *c.* 1750.
Formerly in the collections of the Rev. E. Gardiner, Mrs. Harward of Clevedon, Somerset, and D. H. Carstairs, New York.
Coll.: *Rt. Hon. Sir Philip Sassoon, Bart., M.P., London.*

LELY, SIR PETER
(1618–1680)

4. THE FAMILY OF THE ARTIST.
    Oil, 46×91¾ inches.
The artist is seen playing a bass-viol. On his right are his two children, on his left four representations of his wife Ursula in different attitudes.
Formerly in the collection of Lord Methuen, Corsham Court.
Coll.: *Viscount Lee of Fareham, White Lodge, Richmond.*

DANCKERTS, HENRY
(1630–1678)

5. 'THE PINEAPPLE PICTURE.'
> Oil.

On the back of the picture's frame is the following note in Horace Walpole's writing: 'Mr. Rose, the royal Gardener presenting to King Charles 2^d the first pineapple raised in England. The picture belonged to Mr. London, the nurseryman (partner of Mr. Wise) whose Heir bequeathed it to the Revd. Mr. Pennicott of Ditton, who gave it to Mr. Walpole 1780. Hor. Walpole.' In the catalogue of the Strawberry Hill Collection, which Walpole compiled in 1784, he describes the painting as 'a most curious picture of Rose, the Royal gardener, presenting the first pineapple raised in England to Charles II, who is standing in the garden; the house seems to be Dawney Court, near Windsor, the villa of the Duchess of Cleveland. The whole piece is well painted, probably by Dankers.' Mr. Lionel Cust doubts the correctness of the attribution to Danckerts and suggests that the two figures are the work of Michael Wright (died *c.* 1700). The landscape according to Major Benton Fletcher represents Dawnay Court, Surrey, which belonged to Charles II and where the old pine-pits were still in existence until a few years ago.

Replicas of the picture are in the collections of H.M. the Queen at Windsor, of the Earl of Dysart at Ham House, Petersham, and of Lord Harlech.

Former collections: Sixth Earl Waldegrave, Henry Labouchère, Lord Taunton of Quintock Lodge, nr. Bridgwater (sold 1920).

Coll.: *Rt. Hon. Sir Philip Sassoon, Bart., M.P., London.*

HOGARTH, WILLIAM
(1697–1764)

6. TRADE CARD FOR MARY AND ANN HOGARTH.
> Engraving, $6\frac{3}{4} \times 4\frac{3}{4}$ inches (also $4\frac{1}{8} \times 3\frac{5}{8}$ inches).

The inscription under the engraving reads: 'From the old Frock Shop the corner of the Long Walk facing the Cloysters. Removed to Y^e *King's Arms* joyning to y^e Little Britain Gate near Long Walk.'

Mary and Ann Hogarth were the artist's sisters. Little Britain was famous for its book shops.

> Signed: Hogarth del: T. Cook Sculpt.

WOOTTON, JOHN
(1686(?)–1765)

7. MEMBERS OF THE BEAUFORT HUNT.
> Oil, 78×95 inches.

In the centre, on horseback, is George Henry, third Earl of Lichfield (1718–1772); on the left, holding a gun, is his uncle, the Hon. Robert Lee (1706–1776), who became the fourth Earl. They are both wearing the blue coats of the Beaufort Hunt.

> Painted in 1744.

> Coll.: *The National Gallery, Millbank.*

8. THE BEAUCHAMP AND RIVERS FAMILIES AND SIR NEVIL HICKMAN.
> Oil.

In the carriage are Lady Beauchamp, Lady Rivers and Miss Beauchamp (afterwards Lady Bacon). Standing by the horse in the centre of the picture is Lord Rivers. The two gentlemen on horseback on the right are Sir W. P. Beauchamp and Sir Nevil Hickman.

We have been unable to ascertain the present ownership of the picture.

HEIDELOFF, NIKOLAUS WILHELM
(Born 1761)

9. A COLOURED AQUATINT FROM *Gallery of Fashion*. (*See Fig. 2.*)

'Two Ladies en négligé, taking an airing in a Phaeton,' a plate from the August, 1794, issue.

HILL, DAVID OCTAVIUS
(1802–1870)

10. PHOTOGRAPH TAKEN IN EDINBURGH DURING THE EARLY 'FORTIES.

FOX-TALBOT, WILLIAM HENRY
(1800–1877)

11. PHOTOGRAPH TAKEN ABOUT 1842, PROBABLY AT LACOCK ABBEY.

HOGARTH, WILLIAM
(1697–1764)

12. THE WEDDING OF MR. STEPHEN BECKINGHAM AND MISS MARY COX OF KIDDERMINSTER.
Oil, 50×40⅝ inches.

Stephen Beckingham, of Lincoln's Inn (died 1756), married as his first wife Mary Cox of Kidderminster (died 1738). As given in the Parish Register the marriage took place on June 9th, 1729, at St. Benet's, Paul's Wharf, the Rector, 'Tho. Cooke,' officiating. Yet, as Dr. G. C. Williamson has pointed out, the architectural details, if not the actual plan of the building, put it beyond doubt that the church interior depicted by Hogarth is that of St. Martin's-in-the-Fields.

Signed and dated: *Nuptiae S^th Beckingham A.V. June 9th 1729, Wm. Hogarth pinx^t.*

Formerly in the collections of Herbert William Deedes, Esq., of Saltwood Castle, Kent, and the late Mr. James Carstairs, New York.

Coll.: *The Knoedler Galleries.*

13. SCENE FROM 'THE INDIAN EMPEROR.'
Oil, 50×56 inches.

The painting depicts a performance of Dryden's 'The Indian Emperor; or the Conquest of Mexico,' which took place in 1731 in the house of Mr. Conduit, Master of the Mint. The names of the people represented are recorded in a keyplate in *Hogarth Illustrated*, 1793, Vol. II, page 331. They are: The Duke of Cumberland, Princess Mary, Princess Louisa, Lady Deloraine and her daughters, the Duke and Duchess of Richmond, the Earl of Pomfret, the Duke of Montague, Tom Hill, Captain Poyntz and Doctor Desaguliers. The child-actors are: Lord Lempster as Cortes, Lady Caroline Lenox as Cydara, Lady Sophia Fermor as Almeria and Miss Conduit, afterwards Lady Lymington, as Alibech.

Formerly in the collection of the Earl of Upper Ossory.

Coll.: *Mary, Countess of Ilchester, Holland House, London.*

14. THE WESTERN FAMILY.
Oil, 28¼×33 inches.

At the table are sitting Mrs. Western, with her little daughter next to her; on her right are her son and his wife, on her left the Rev. William Hatsell and a servant.

Signed: W. Hogarth 173–? (*c.* 1735).

Formerly in the collections of Lord Western, of Rivenhall, Essex, Sir Thomas Western and Sir Hugh Lane.

Coll.: *The National Gallery of Ireland, Dublin.*

15. THE GRAHAM CHILDREN.

Oil, 64×71 inches.

Believed to represent the children of Robert Bontine Cunningham Graham, of Gartmore, and to have been painted in 1742.

From the collections of R. R. Graham of Chelsea (until 1814), William Seguier, G. Watson Taylor, the Earl of Normanton (who purchased the picture for ninety guineas).

Coll.: *The National Gallery, London.*

16. THE CHOLMONDELEY FAMILY.

Oil, 29½×38 inches.

George, third Earl of Cholmondeley, with his wife and their three elder children. The man standing behind the Earl's chair has not been identified.

Signed and dated: *W. Hogarth. 1732 Pinx^t.*

Coll.: *The Marquess of Cholmondeley, London.*

17. A FAMILY PARTY.

Oil, 21×29½ inches.

Coll.: *Sir Herbert Cook, Bart., Doughty House, Richmond.*

18. TASTE IN HIGH LIFE.

Oil, 25×30 inches.

The man on the right is said to be Lord Portmore, and the black boy on the left Ignatius Sancho. The identity of the women is unknown. One of the pictures on the wall represents Desnoyer, the dancing master. The picture of Venus in the centre bears the date 1642. The painting, which is meant to caricature the fashions of the time, was commissioned by a Miss Edwardes in 1742. It was engraved without Hogarth's permission in 1746.

Coll.: *The Earl of Iveagh, London.*

19. THE BROTHERS CLARKE, OF SWAKELEYS, ROUND A TABLE TAKING WINE.

Oil, 32×45 inches.

Thomas Clarke and his brother are the two principal figures in the group. Thomas Clarke purchased the property Swakeleys, situated at Ickenham, Middlesex, in 1750, and it is very likely that the picture was made at the time of the transfer, as one of the personages is apparently a lawyer. There is the following entry in a diary of 1822 written by John Hughes, who married Thomas Clarke's daughter: 'Rowland brings home Mrs. Hughes' family picture by Hogarth superbly framed in oil gilding, etc.' The painting remained in the Hughes family until 1933.

Coll.: *The Tooth Galleries.*

20. A FAMILY GROUP.

Oil, 34×35 inches.

From left to right: Dr. Arthur Smith, who was Archbishop of Dublin from 1766 to 1772; William Strode; Jonathan Powell, Strode's butler; Lady Anne Strode, William Strode's mother, the daughter of the fifth Earl of Salisbury; S. Strode.

Formerly owned by the Rev. W. Finch, who bequeathed the picture to the National Gallery in 1883.

Coll.: *The National Gallery, London.*

21. THE PRICE FAMILY.

Oil, 40¼×62½ inches.

The setting is on the Price estate at Foxley, Herefordshire. Uvedale Tomkyns Price is seen on the landing steps helping his cousin, Miss Rodd, to alight. On the left his son Robert is talking with Miss Greville, another cousin; Esther Greville is feeding the swans.

Coll.: *The Metropolitan Museum, New York.*

22. THE BROKEN FAN.
>   Oil, 26×27 inches.

The figures are believed to be, from left to right, Lady Thornhill, her daughter, Hogarth's wife, and the artist's sister. The fact that Lady Thornhill is wearing widow's clothes allows one to assume that the picture was painted soon after 1734, when Sir James Thornhill died.
>   Coll.: *Lord Northbrook.*

23. PORTRAIT GROUP OF A FISHING PARTY.
>   Oil, 21¾×18½ inches.
>   Coll.: *The Dulwich Gallery.*

24. CONVERSATION GROUP.
>   Pen and ink over red chalk, washed with Indian ink and water colour, 12¾×17¼ inches.

Formerly in the William Russell and the Cheney collections.
>   Coll.: *The British Museum, London.*

UNIDENTIFIED ARTIST
(Eighteenth Century)

25. A FAMILY GROUP.
>   Oil, 42¼×54 inches.
>   Coll.: *Lady Hudson, G.B.E., Downshire House, Roehampton.*

UNIDENTIFIED ARTIST
(c. 1720)

26. AN ENGLISH PARTY.
>   Oil, 39⅛×45¾ inches.
>   Coll.: *The National Gallery, London.*

HOGARTH, WILLIAM
(1697–1764)

27. LORD GEORGE GRAHAM IN HIS CABIN.
>   Oil, 28×35 inches.

Lord George Graham was the fourth son of the fourth Marquess and first Duke of Montrose. He was born in 1715.
>   Formerly in the collection of the Duke of Montrose.
>   Coll.: *The National Maritime Museum, Greenwich.*

ZOFFANY, JOHN, R.A.
(1733–1810)

28. QUEEN CHARLOTTE AND HER TWO ELDER CHILDREN.
>   Oil, 40×50 inches.

Queen Charlotte is seen in her dressing room at old Buckingham Palace. With her are George Augustus, Prince of Wales (born 1762) in Roman military costume, and Frederick, Duke of York and Albany (born 1763) in Oriental attire. The French clock by the door now stands near the picture at Windsor Castle.

There is some uncertainty about the identity of the child in Oriental dress, who has also been stated to be the Princess Royal (born 1766).

One of a series of four paintings executed for Queen Charlotte, c. 1766–1767.
>   Coll.: *His Majesty the King, Windsor Castle.*

29. THE DUTTON FAMILY.
     Oil, 40½ × 50¼ inches.

The second figure from the left represents James Lenox Naper (died 1776) of Loughcrew, Meath, son of James Naper and Anne, daughter of Sir Ralph Dutton, first Baronet; he assumed in consequence the surname and arms of Dutton. His second wife Jane, daughter of Christopher Bond of Newland, Gloucestershire, is on the right next to her eldest son James (1744–1820), who became first Lord Sherborne. The lady on the left is Mr. and Mrs. Dutton's fourth daughter Jane (died 1800), who married in 1775 Thomas Coke, of Holkham, afterwards Earl of Leicester.

The interior represents the drawing-room at Sherborne Park, Gloucestershire.

Formerly in the possession of Lord Sherborne.

Coll.: *Daniel H. Farr, Esq., U.S.A.*

30. JOHN, THIRD DUKE OF ATHOLL, AND HIS FAMILY ON THE BANKS OF THE TAY AT DUNKELD.
     Oil, 36 × 63 inches.

John Murray, third Duke of Atholl (1729–1774), married Lady Charlotte Murray and had seven sons and four daughters. The eldest son, John, who became the fourth Duke, is seen by his father's side.

The painting was commissioned by the Duke as an overmantel decoration for a room in Blair Castle. A receipt from Zoffany dated 'London, 16th Jan., 1767' states: 'Received from the Duke of Atholl Eighty-nine Pounds which with One Hundred Pounds formerly Receivd Makes in All One Hundred and Eighty Guineys, being in full for a Family Picture of Nine Figures at Twenty Guineys Each.' According to Dr. G. C. Williamson, 'the background, which represents the Tay and the hill Craig Venian, with the Atholl Cairn, appears to be the work of Charles Stewart (brother of Anthony Stewart, 1773–1846, the miniature painter), who was at that time on Tayside, painting for the Duke of Atholl a series of landscapes which now form five panels in the dining-room, and are signed by him and dated 1766, 1767, 1768, 1777 and 1778. It would appear that the canvas, having been prepared for the exact place in the room, had the landscape painted upon it by Stewart, and then was brought up to London so that Zoffany could carry out his work from sittings when the members of the family were in town.'

Signed '*Johan Zoffany*,' and dated 1767.

The picture was begun in 1765 and first exhibited at the Society of Artists in 1769.

Coll.: *The Duke of Atholl, Blair Castle, Blair-Atholl.*

31. THE COWPER AND GORE FAMILIES.
     Oil, 30 × 38 inches.

The figures from left to right are: Lady Cowper; her sister, Emily Gore; her father, Charles Gore; Earl Cowper; another sister of Lady Cowper; her mother, Lady Gore. George, third Earl Cowper (1738–1789), married Hannah Anne Gore in Florence in 1775. Charles Gore, of Horkstow, Lincolnshire, is said to have been the prototype of the 'travelled Englishman' in Goethe's 'Wilhelm Meister.'

The picture was painted at the Villa Palmieri in Florence for Earl Cowper. It was lost, probably stolen, after Lady Cowper's death in 1826, but was discovered in 1845 in an antique shop in Florence and bought by the family for twenty pounds.

Coll.: *Lady Desborough, Panshanger.*

32. A MUSICAL PARTY ON THE THAMES.
     Oil, 45 × 49 inches.

The painting depicts the Sharp family on their pleasure barge at Fulham. On top, by the steering wheel, is William Sharp, surgeon to King George III. Next to him stands Dr. John Sharp's daughter, Anna Jemima. Seated below them are Catharine, wife of James Sharp, *née* Lodge; Catharine, wife of William Sharp, *née* Berwick, with her only child Mary (afterwards Mrs. T. J. Lloyd-Baker); Judith Sharp—playing the lute. In front from left to right are: James Sharp, an engineer; his daughter Catharine; Granville Sharp, the philanthropist; Elizabeth Prowse, widow of George Prowse of Wichen Park, Northampton and Berkeley; Frances Sharp, the youngest sister; Dr. John Sharp, Prebendary of Durham, Archdeacon of Northumberland and Almoner to Queen Anne—the eldest brother; his wife, Mary, *née* Dering. In the left corner at the back are the boatmaster and the cabin-boy, who was still alive in 1848 and from whom the above identification of the portrayals has been derived. In the foreground lies Zoffany's dog, Roma. The view is of Fulham, with the church and a villa owned by the Sharps.

The picture was commissioned by William Sharp and is said to have cost eight hundred guineas. It was first exhibited at the Royal Academy in 1781, when Horace Walpole wrote about it: 'The figures are most natural, and highly finished, but a great want of keeping on the whole.'

Coll.: *Miss Olive Lloyd-Baker, Hardwick Court, Gloucester.*

33. THE TRIBUNA.
Oil, 47×59 inches.
Group on left: Earl Cowper, Sir John Dick, Earl of Plymouth, Zoffany, Stevenson, Earl of Dartmouth, Lord Russborough, Valentine Knightley, Lorain Smith—seated, sketching with Lord Mount Edgcumbe watching him. In the centre is Bianchi, seated in the foreground—the Hon. Felton Hervey. Group on right: Gordon, Patch, Sir John Taylor, Sir Horace Mann, Earl of Winchelsea, Watts, Doughty, T. Wilbraham. On the extreme right are Bruce and Wilbraham. The interior represents the Tribuna at the Uffizi in Florence. The picture which is seen next to the head of Zoffany is the famous 'Cowper Madonna' by Raphael, which Zoffany discovered and sold to Earl Cowper. It is now in the Widener Collection, Philadelphia.

Painted in Florence. First exhibited at the Royal Academy in 1780 and subsequently purchased by Queen Charlotte.

Coll.: *His Majesty the King, Windsor.*

34. THE AURIOL FAMILY.
Oil, 56×78 inches.
Seated in the centre are Charlotte Auriol, who became Mrs. Thomas Dashwood, and her sister Sophia, who married John Prinsep. Next to her sits Thomas Dashwood, second son of Sir James Dashwood of Kirklington, Oxford, and next to him stands James Auriol. The men in the group on the left are Charles Auriol, John Auriol and John Prinsep. The other four figures are native servants.

Painted in India between 1783 and 1789.

Coll.: *M. G. Dashwood, Esq., The Pré, St. Albans.*

35. THE HEATLY GROUP.
Oil, 40×45 inches.
Suetonius Grant Heatly, a judge in the service of the East India Company and Magistrate for the province of Dana, with his sister Temperance, who afterwards married Captain William Green, R.N. With them is a pipe-bearer (standing in the back) and a servant or messenger.

Painted in India between 1783 and 1789.

Coll.: *Captain Blunt, C.D.M., of Adderbury Manor, Banbury, and Miss J. H. Blunt.*

36. A FAMILY GROUP.
Oil, 40×50 inches.
The group is supposed to represent a Mrs. Bruere and her children, and to have belonged to Colonel Claud Martin, the founder of the Martinière College at Lucknow.

Bequeathed by William Asch in 1922.

Coll.: *The National Gallery, London.*

37. Charles Towneley and his Friends in his Library.
   Oil, 61×49 inches.

Charles Towneley (1737–1805), the famous collector of classical antiques, is on the right of the picture. The group in the background is formed by Dankerville (seated), Charles Greville and Sir Thomas Astle. The interior represents Towneley's library at 7 Park Street, Westminster (now 14 Queen Anne's Gate). Most of the marbles which Zoffany had brought from different parts of the house into the library when he was painting the picture are now in the British Museum. Nollekens mentions in his diary that 'the likeness of Mr. Towneley is extremely good. He looks like the dignified possessor of such treasures. At his feet lies his faithful dog Kam, a native of Kamtchatka, whose mother was one of the dogs yoked to the sledge which drew Captain King to that island.'
   Originally exhibited at the Royal Academy in 1790.
   Coll.: *Lord O'Hagan.*

38. The Garricks entertaining Dr. Johnson.
   Oil, 38½×48½ inches.

Dr. Johnson, Mr. and Mrs. David Garrick, Mr. Bowden and Mr. George Garrick (fishing) in the grounds of the actor's villa at Hampton. The lady in the picture has also been described as Mrs. Bowden and Mrs. Thrale.
   A companion piece to Fig. 39.
   Sold at Garrick's sale to the second Earl of Durham for £25.
   Coll.: *The Earl of Durham, Lambton Castle.*

39. Mr. and Mrs. Garrick at Shakespeare's Temple at Hampton.
   Oil, 39×49 inches.

David Garrick (1717–1779), the actor, married Eve Marie Violetti (1724–1824), who was presumably the daughter of a Viennese called Viegel. The large St. Bernard dog must be 'Dragon' to whom an ode was dedicated by Hannah More. 'Shakespeare's Temple,' also called 'Pope's Villa,' was built in the grounds of Garrick's villa at Hampton about 1756 by Adam. In it stood a statue of Shakespeare by Roubiliac, which was bequeathed by Garrick to the British Museum.
   A companion piece to Fig. 38.
   Sold at Garrick's sale to the second Earl of Durham for £25.
   Coll.: *The Earl of Durham, Lambton Castle.*

40. The Colmore Family.
   Oil, 39½×50 inches.
   Coll.: *Rt. Hon. Sir Philip Sassoon, Bart., M.P., London.*

41. Captain John Augustus Hervey taking Leave of his Family on Appointment to the Command of a Ship.
   Oil, 39½×49 inches.

From left to right: Lord and Lady Mulgrave, Lady Mary Fitzgerald, Mr. George Fitzgerald, Captain Hervey and his wife.
   John Augustus Hervey (1724–1779) became the third Earl of Bristol in 1775 and a vice-admiral in 1778. Constantine John Phipps, second Baron Mulgrave (1744–1792) was in command of the *Racehorse* on a polar expedition in 1773, of which he published an account.
   Coll.: *The Marquess of Bristol, Ickworth, Bury St. Edmunds.*

42. A Man and Two Boys, One with a Kite.
   Oil, 39×49 inches.
   Exhibited by Zoffany at the Society of Artists in 1764 under the title 'A Family.'
   Coll.: *Sir Sidney Herbert, Bart.*

43. MR. AND MRS. BLEW AND FAMILY.
    Oil, 29¼×31¼ inches.
Formerly in the collection of Lady Mount Stephen.
Coll.: *Lady Hudson, G.B.E., Downshire House, Roehampton.*

44. LORD WILLOUGHBY DE BROKE AND HIS FAMILY.
    Oil, 39½×49¼ inches.
John, fourteenth Lord Willoughby de Broke married Lady Louisa North, daughter of Francis, first Earl of Guildford and sister of Lord North. The three children are John, the fifteenth Baron; Henry, who succeeded to the title on his brother's death; and Louisa, who married the Rev. Albert Barnard, Prebendary of Winchester.
The setting represents the breakfast-room at Compton Verney. The silver tea-urn, which is seen on the table, still remains in the possession of the family.
Coll.: *Lord Willoughby de Broke, Woodley House, Kineton.*

45. THE DRUMMOND FAMILY AT CADLAND.
    Oil, 58×94 inches.
The picture represents Robert Drummond with his wife and children on the coast at Cadland, overlooking the Solent.
Robert was a nephew of Andrew Drummond, the banker, who with his family form the subjects of another group by Zoffany, now in the possession of George H. Drummond, Esq., London.
Formerly in the collection of Lord Wandsworth.
Coll.: *The Hon. Mrs. Ionides.*

46. THE FAMILY OF SIR WILLIAM YOUNG.
    Oil, 44×66½ inches.
Sir William Young was created Baronet in 1769 and was sometime Governor of St. Vincent and of Dominica. His eldest son William (1749–1815), seen on the right with one of his sisters, became second Baronet and was later Governor of Tobago.
In Lady Young's collection there exist two separate replicas of the groups on the left and on the right of this picture.
From the collection of Sir William Young, Bart.
Coll.: *Rt. Hon. Sir Philip Sassoon, Bart., M.P., London.*

47. SIR LAWRENCE DUNDAS WITH HIS GRANDSON LAWRENCE.
    Oil, 40×50 inches.
The child Lawrence (born 1766) was the son of Thomas, eldest son of Sir Lawrence Dundas, and was created first Earl of Zetland in 1838.
The interior represents a room in 19 Arlington Street. The furniture and *objets d'art*, as well as the painting by Van der Capelle, which is seen over the mantelpiece, still remain in the possession of the family.
Coll.: *The Marquess of Zetland, Aske, Richmond, Yorkshire.*

48. THE SONS OF JOHN, THIRD EARL OF BUTE.
    Oil, 30×48 inches.
The picture represents three of the sons of John, third Earl of Bute. One of them is William Stuart (1755–1822), who became Archbishop of Armagh in 1800. The others are probably Sir Charles Stuart (1753–1801), who followed a military career, and Frederick (1751–1802), later M.P. for Bute.
A companion piece to Fig. 49.
Coll.: *The Marquess of Bute.*

49. DAUGHTERS OF JOHN, THIRD EARL OF BUTE.
     Oil, 30×48 inches.

A companion piece to Fig. 48.
Coll.: *The Marquess of Bute.*

50. A FAMILY PARTY: THE MINUET.
     Oil, 39×49 inches.

Purchased from the McLellan Gallery in 1854.
Coll.: *The Corporation Gallery, Glasgow.*

51. ZOFFANY AND HIS FAMILY.
     Oil, 30×42 inches.

According to family tradition the picture, which has always remained in the possession of the artist's descendants, represents Zoffany, his five children and their old nurse, Mrs. Ann Chase. The presence of five children, when Zoffany never had more than four alive at the same time, is variously explained by the two suggestions that the baby in the nurse's arms is an imaginary portrait of the artist's son who died in infancy, or that his third daughter Claudina has been represented twice. Dr. G. C. Williamson's suggestion that the lady at the harpsichord may be Mrs. Zoffany hardly solves the problem considering that Zoffany's daughters were born in 1777, 1780, 1793 and 1795 respectively, the difference of age between the second and third thus being thirteen years which is contrary to their appearance in the picture. Another possibility would be that the baby in arms is a grandchild of Zoffany—a son or a daughter of his daughter Cecilia who married the Rev. Thomas Horne in 1799. In this case the picture would have been painted in 1801 or later, a date which corresponds with the looks of all the portrayed personages.
Coll.: *Mrs. O. Benwell.*

DEVIS, ARTHUR
(*c.* 1711–1787)

52. SIR JOSHUA VANNECK AND HIS FAMILY.
     Oil, 56½×56 inches.

From left to right the gentlemen in the picture are: Sir Joshua Vanneck, the Hon. Thomas Walpole, Master Gerald Vanneck, Master Joshua Vanneck (afterwards first Lord Huntingfield) and Horace Walpole. The ladies are: Mrs. De La Mont and Elizabeth, Anna Maria and Gertrude Vanneck. The young girl seated on the ground is Margaret Vanneck who later married the Hon. Richard Walpole.
Signed and dated 1752.
Formerly in the collection of Lady Dorothy Nevill.
Coll.: *Miss Frick, Pride's Crossing, Mass., U.S.A.*

53. AN INCIDENT IN THE GROUNDS OF RANELAGH DURING A BAL MASQUÉ.
     Oil, 50×40 inches.

The picture is said to commemorate an incident in the life of William Henry Ricketts and his wife Mary, a sister of Admiral Sir John Jervis, Earl of St. Vincent. Mr. and Mrs. Ricketts met at a fancy dress ball at Ranelagh without recognising one another under their disguise. Only when, yielding to a strong mutual attraction, they agreed to take off their masks, did they discover their identity.
Coll.: *Lieut.-Colonel W. S. W. Parker-Jervis, D.S.O.*

54. THE TILL FAMILY.
      Oil, 42×62 inches.

Mr. Stacey Till is standing on the right with his son John and his daughter Sarah. On the garden seat is Mrs. Stacey Till with her youngest child Richard and her brother, Mr. Edward Gilbert.

Stacey Till (1716–1785) was the son of John Till of Ongar, Essex, and married in 1743 Sarah Gilbert (1719–1799), elder daughter of William Gilbert, attorney at law. Their eldest son John (1744–1827) was vicar of Hayes, Kent, where he is buried; their daughter Sarah (1745–1830) married the Rev. Launcelot Sharpe, and their son Richard (1749–1823) was married in 1774 to Elizabeth Weddale of Aldgate.

From the collection of Mrs. Slade (*née* Till).

Coll.: *Sir Herbert Hughes-Stanton, R.A., London.*

UNIDENTIFIED ARTIST

(Once erroneously attributed to Arthur W. Devis)

55. THE PUTNAM FAMILY.
      Oil, 41½×33½ inches.

On a column in the centre of the picture hangs a shield, the right half of which has been identified as the arms of the Sussex branch of the Putnam family. The Putnams of Sussex emigrated to America in the eighteenth century or earlier.

Coll.: *The Knoedler Galleries.*

DEVIS, ARTHUR

(c. 1711–1787)

56. HORACE WALPOLE PRESENTING KITTY CLIVE WITH A PIECE OF HONEYSUCKLE.
      Oil, 28×36 inches.

Kitty Clive (1711–1785), the actress, was a great friend of Horace Walpole (1717–1797). He presented her with a house at Strawberry Hill, jokingly called by Garrick 'Clive's-den,' where she retired in 1769 and where she died. The view in the picture was probably taken from the house.

Coll.: *Lady Margaret Douglas.*

57. PORTRAIT OF A GENTLEMAN AND TWO LADIES.
      Oil, 25×30 inches.

It has been suggested that the large mansion in the background might possibly be Syon House.

Coll.: *Sir Herbert Hughes-Stanton, R.A., London.*

58. MR. AND MRS. RICHARD BULL OF NORTHCOURT.
      Oil, 42×34 inches.

Richard Bull, a Turkey merchant of the City of London, was a friend of Horace Walpole and a great collector of old engravings and books.

Signed and dated 1742.

Formerly in the collections of Mr. Richard Bull, General Sir James Willoughby Gordon, G.C.M.G., and Lord Burgh.

Coll.: *Jesse Isidor Strauss, Esq., New York.*

59. THE SEFTON FAMILY.
      Oil, 36×49¼ inches.

Though known as 'The Sefton Family,' the picture probably represents members of the Molyneux family, ancestors of the Earls of Sefton. It was painted at Hawkley Hall, Pemberton, Lancashire.

Formerly owned by Bryan William Hockenhall Molyneux, M.A., D.C.L., of Onibury, Salop (born 1852), a grandson of William Hockenhall who took the surname of Molyneux by Royal Licence in 1805, in accordance with the will of Bryan Molyneux of Hawkley Hall, Pemberton, whose estates he inherited.
Coll.: *The Knoedler Galleries.*

STUBBS, GEORGE, A.R.A.
(1724–1806)

60. COLONEL POCKLINGTON AND HIS SISTERS.
    Oil, 38¾×48¾ inches.
Signed and dated: *Geo. Stubbs pinxit* 1769.
Coll.: *Mrs. Charles Carstairs.*

61. THE THIRD DUKE OF PORTLAND ON A WHITE HORSE.
    Oil, 38¾×48¾ inches.
William Henry Cavendish Bentinck, third Duke of Portland (1738–1809) was a prominent statesman and sportsman. The building represents the Welbeck riding school.
Signed: *Geo. Stubbs pinxit.* First exhibited at the Society of Artists in 1767. A companion piece to Fig. 62.
Coll.: *The Duke of Portland, Welbeck Abbey.*

62. THE THIRD DUKE OF PORTLAND AND HIS BROTHER, LORD EDWARD BENTINCK.
    Oil, 39×49 inches.
Signed: *George Stubbs pinxit.*
Companion piece to Fig. 61.
Coll.: *The Duke of Portland, Welbeck Abbey.*

63. THE MELBOURNE AND MILBANKE FAMILIES.
    Oil, 38¼×58¾ inches.
In the carriage is Lady Melbourne; her father, Sir Ralph Milbanke of Halnaby, Yorkshire, stands beside her; Lord Melbourne is in the centre and Mr. John Milbanke is on the right.
Peniston Lamb, first Viscount Melbourne (1748–1819) married in 1769 Elizabeth Milbanke (1749–1818). On her death Byron referred to her as 'the best, and kindest, and ablest female I have ever known, old or young.'
From the collection of Earl Cowper.
Coll.: *Lady Desborough, Panshanger.*

64. JOSIAH WEDGWOOD AND HIS FAMILY.
    Oil, 47¾×72½ inches.
Josiah Wedgwood (1730–1795), the famous potter, married in 1764 Sarah (1734–1815), daughter of Richard Wedgwood of Spen Green and his cousin in the third degree. They had seven children, all of whom appear in the picture. The eldest daughter, Sussannah, later married Robert Waring Darwin, the father of Charles Robert Darwin, and the third son, Thomas, became famous as a pioneer of photography.
Painted in 1780.
Coll.: *Mrs. Cecil Wedgwood, Cheadle.*

65. PHAETON AND PAIR.
    Oil on wood, 32×39 inches.
Signed and dated: *Geo. Stubbs pinxit* 1787.
Coll.: *The National Gallery, London.*

66. THE PRINCE OF WALES' PHAETON AND STATE COACHMEN.
    Oil, 40×50¼ inches.
Painted in 1793.
Formerly at Carlton House.
Coll.: *His Majesty the King, Windsor.*

GAINSBOROUGH, THOMAS, R.A.
(1727–1788)

67. HENEAGE LLOYD AND HIS SISTER.
    Oil, 25×31½ inches.
    Signed in monogram: *T. G.* Painted between 1752 and 1759.
Formerly in the collections of Lieut.-Colonel Anstruther and C. Fairfax Murray, who
presented the picture to the Fitzwilliam Museum in 1911.
Coll.: *The Fitzwilliam Museum, Cambridge.*

68. PORTRAIT OF A LADY AND GENTLEMAN.
    Oil, 29¼×25⅜ inches.
The style in which the picture is painted suggests that it was executed about the same
time as the Kirby portrait in the National Portrait Gallery (Fig. 69).
Coll.: *The Dulwich Gallery.*

69. JOHN JOSHUA KIRBY AND SARAH BULL, HIS WIFE.
    Oil, 29¼×24¼ inches.
John Joshua Kirby, F.R.S. (1716–1774), painter, writer on linear perspective and President
of the Incorporated Society of Artists, was a friend of Gainsborough from the time of his
youth.
An early work.
Coll.: *The National Portrait Gallery, London.*

70. MR. AND MRS. BROWN, OF TRENT HALL.
    Oil, 33×55½ inches.
Mr. Brown of Ipswich owned an estate at Tunstall, Suffolk, where the picture was probably
painted. If the child is correctly assumed to be Anna Maria Brown, who was born in 1753, it
puts the date of the picture about 1756.
Formerly in the collections of Colonel F. B. Longe and Viscount d'Abernon.
Coll.: *Rt. Hon. Sir Philip Sassoon, Bart., M.P., London.*

71. ROBERT ANDREWS AND HIS WIFE.
    Oil, 27½×47 inches.
An early work (*c.* 1755), which was painted at Auberies, near Sudbury, Suffolk.
Coll.: *G. W. Andrews, Esq., Ashtead.*

WARD, JAMES, R.A.
(1769–1859)

72. THE HALL PLUMER FAMILY.
    Oil, 48×31⅞ inches.
Hall Plumer was the brother of Sir Thomas Plumer (1753–1824), the great-grandfather
of the late Field-Marshal Lord Plumer. The scenery represents Hall Plumer's country seat,
Bilton Hall, Yorkshire, where the picture hung from the time it was painted, *c.* 1790, until 1934.
Coll.: *The Knoedler Galleries.*

COTES, FRANCIS, R.A.
(1726–1770)

73. MR. AND MRS. BENNETT AND THEIR TWO DAUGHTERS.
    Oil, 43 × 34 inches.
    Formerly owned by Miss Spence and the Rev. Daw Bennett.
    Coll.: *Sir Herbert Hughes-Stanton, R.A., London.*

HAMILTON, GAWEN
(c. 1697–1737)

74. THE EARL OF STRAFFORD AND HIS FAMILY.
    Oil, 33⅛ × 37 inches.
    Portraits of Thomas Wentworth, first Earl of Strafford, wearing the insignia of the Garter; of his wife; their daughters, Ladies Anne, Lucy and Henrietta Wentworth; and their only son, Lord Wentworth. The picture was painted in the Earl's house at 5 St. James's Square, S.W. Over the arch leading to the staircase is his arms with the motto 'En Dieu est Tout.'
    Thomas Wentworth, first Earl of Strafford (1672–1739), was a distinguished soldier who took part in most of Marlborough's campaigns. Later, in 1706 and 1711 respectively, he was ambassador at Berlin and at The Hague. He married Anne, daughter of Sir Henry Johnson, Knt., of Bradenham, Bucks., and had three daughters and one son: Anne who married the Rt. Hon. William Conolly; Lucy who married Field-Marshal Sir George Howard, K.B.; Henrietta who married Henry Vernon of Hilton; William (1722–1791) who succeeded his father in 1739.
    In Vertue's manuscript at the British Museum, written about June 1732, is the following reference to this picture: 'a family piece of the present Earl of Strafford himself his Lady, his son and daughters in the Conversation manner, the dispo[si]tion genteel and agreable— the Countenances like and freely pencilld, draperys Silks. and decorations well toucht and disposed. upon the whole, this is esteemed a master peace of Mr. Hamiltons painting. who [? as] much like Hogarths works as can be. & this he did for Reputation being the Earls great generosity to give him ten guineas only for it.'
    Signed '*G. Hamilton*' and dated 1732.
    From the collection of Captain B. C. Vernon-Wentworth of Wentworth Castle, Barnsley, Yorkshire.
    Coll.: *The Heirs of the late D. H. Carstairs, New York.*

75. A CLUB OF ARTISTS.
    Oil, 34 × 43 inches.
    In the centre of the picture is Matthew Robinson (died 1778) of West Layton, Yorkshire, for whom the painting was made in 1735. The other figures from left to right are: George Vertue (1684–1756), engraver; Hans Huyssing (died c. 1740), Swedish portrait painter; Michael Dahl (1656–1743), Swedish portrait painter; William Thomas, architect; James Gibbs, architect; Joseph Goupy (c. 1700–1763), French painter and engraver; Charles Bridgeman, landscape gardener, who laid out the Serpentine and Kensington Gardens; Bernard Baron (c. 1700–1766), French engraver; John Wootton (c. 1686–1765), painter; John Michael Rysbrack (c. 1693–1770), sculptor; Gawen Hamilton; William Kent (1684–1748), architect.
    In a note preserved in the British Museum Vertue describes the picture as a 'Conversation of Virtuosi that usually meat at the Kings Armes, new bond street, a noted tavern.' The same manuscript contains the key of the personages represented.
    Coll.: *The National Portrait Gallery, London.*

LAROON, MARCELLUS
(1679–1772)

76. A MUSICAL CONVERSATION.
> Oil, 25×30 inches.
> Coll.: *Sir Alec Martin, London.*

77. THE DUKE OF BUCKINGHAM'S LEVÉE.
> Oil, 37×30 inches.

John Sheffield, third Earl of Mulgrave (1648–1721), was created Duke of Buckingham and Normandy in 1702–1703.

In a catalogue of the collections of Southill Park compiled in 1815 the picture is mentioned as 'The Duke of Buckingham's Levée,' but no painter's name is given. The general opinion of experts that it is a work by Laroon is further supported by the discovery in the British Museum of a sketch by that artist, representing the two figures on the extreme left.
> Coll.: *Samuel Howard Whitbread, Esq., C.B., Southill Park, Biggleswade, Bedfordshire.*

78. A CONCERT AT MONTAGU HOUSE.
> Drawing in pen and ink over pencil, 18×13¼ inches.

A note by Horace Walpole gives the following particulars about this drawing: 'A Concert, by Captain Laroon. The gentleman on the left under the door is John 2nd Duke of Montagu, the lady standing by him is his 2nd daughter Mary Countess of Cardigan afterwards Duchess of Montagu. H.W.' Though Walpole does not mention the name of the musician at the harpsichord, there is no doubt that he is John James Heidegger (1659?–1749), the operatic manager and one time partner of Handel. Heidegger, who was conspicuous by his exceptional ugliness, also appears in another drawing in the British Museum entitled 'Heidegger in a Rage,' attributed to Philip Mercier.
> Signed and dated: *Marcellus Laroon Fecit.* 1736
> Coll.: *The British Museum.*

79. A MUSICAL ASSEMBLY.
> Oil, 40×50 inches.

In a catalogue of the year 1819 in the British Museum the picture is described as 'a Musical Assembly of twenty five figures with the portrait of Frederick, Prince of Wales (the father of our venerable Sovereign), and many of the most distinguished of the nobility and literary characters of the day.' A key etched by Cruikshank gives the following names: Frederick, Prince of Wales; Consort of Frederick, Prince of Wales; Earl of Bute; Lady Pembroke; Princess Amelia Sophia; Lord and Lady Walpole; Princess Caroline Elizabeth; Sir Robert Walpole; Lord Castlemaine; Lord Boyne; Addison; Dr. Young.
> Coll.: *Sir Herbert Hughes-Stanton, R.A., London.*

NOLLEKENS, JOSEPH FRANCIS
(1702–1748)

80. THE MUSIC PARTY.
> Oil, 14×18 inches.

The picture probably depicts a house party at Wanstead House, the seat of Earl Tilney, for whom Nollekens is known to have executed various paintings. Many of the people appear to be the same as in 'A Group of Musicians' in the collection of Mary, Countess of Ilchester. Wanstead House, Essex, now demolished, was a great Palladian mansion built by Colin Campbell.
> Former collections: Humphrey Bowles, Wanstead, and first Lord Northwick.
> Coll.: *Captain E. G. Spencer-Churchill, Northwick Park.*

PHILIPS, CHARLES
(1708–1747)

81. A Garden Party.
    Oil, 29×24¼ inches.
    Coll.: *The National Gallery, Millbank.*

HAMILTON, GAWEN
(*c.* 1697–1737)

82. The Vicar of the Parish at the House of the Infant Squire.
    Oil, 28½×35½ inches.
    Coll.: *Sir Alec Martin, London.*

MERCIER, PHILIP
(1689–1760)

83. A Music Party.
    Oil, 17¼×22½ inches.
    Frederick Lewis, Prince of Wales (1707–1751), eldest son of George II, with his sisters Anne, Princess Royal (1709–1759), who married William, Prince of Orange; Princess Amelia Sophia Eleanora (1711–1786) on the right and Princess Caroline Elizabeth (1713–1757) standing, in the gardens of Kew Palace.
    Painted in 1733.
    Coll.: *The National Portrait Gallery, London.*

SLAUGHTER, STEPHEN
(*c.* 1735–1765)

84. Two Gentlemen Tasting Wine.
    Oil.
    Coll.: *Sir Alec Martin, London.*

HIGHMORE, JOSEPH
(1692–1780)

85. Alexander Pope in his Villa at Twickenham.
    Oil, 30×38 inches.
    A contemporary inscription on the back of the canvas gives the title of the picture, the artist's name, and the date, 1728.
    From the collection of Earl Cowley, Draycott House, Chippenham.
    Coll.: *Private ownership, America.*

HAYMAN, FRANCIS, R.A.
(1708–1776)

86. Three Figures in a Landscape.
    Oil, 41¼×39 inches.
    The group probably represents Margaret and Elizabeth Tyers and either one of their brothers—Thomas or Jonathan—or George Rogers of Southampton, Margaret's husband.

Thomas and Jonathan succeeded their father Jonathan Tyers, who died in 1767, as proprietors of Vauxhall Gardens, the famous pleasure grounds which were opened in 1732. Hayman and Hogarth were employed by Jonathan Tyers, senior, to decorate the supper-boxes and alcoves at Vauxhall. Hayman also painted decorations at Tyers' country house, Denbies, in Sussex, as well as portraits of various members of the Tyers family. These portraits were until recently at Brandon House, the former home of the Rev. Jonathan Tyers Barrett, D.D.
Former collection: Mrs. Boyd Hamilton, Brandon House, Suffolk.
Coll.: *Mrs. Derek Fitzgerald, London.*

87. SIR ROBERT WALPOLE AND FRANCIS HAYMAN, R.A.
Oil, 27¼×35 inches.

Sir Robert Walpole, first Earl of Orford (1676–1745), Prime Minister, in the artist's studio.
Coll.: *The National Portrait Gallery, London.*

BATONI, POMPEO GIROLAMO
(1708–1787)

88. SIR JAMES GRANT, MR. MYTTON, THE HON. THOMAS ROBINSON AND MR. WYNNE.
Oil, 38×48 inches.

Sir James Grant, seventh Baronet (1738–1811), was M.P. for Elgin and Forres from 1761 to 1768, M.P. for Banff from 1790 to 1795 and Lord-Lieutenant of Inverness-shire from 1794–1809. The Hon. Thomas Robinson (1738–1786), who became the second Lord Grantham, was M.P. for Christchurch from 1761 to 1770 and ambassador to the Court of Spain from 1771 to 1779.
Painted in Rome in 1766.
Coll.: *Private ownership, America.*

PATCH, THOMAS
(*c.* 1720–1782)

89. THE DUKE OF ROXBURGHE AND MISS MENDES.
Oil, 23¾×38½ inches.

John Ker, third Duke of Roxburghe (1740–1804), famous book collector, is talking to Patch seated at his easel. Miss Tabitha Mendes, a wealthy Jewess who was a dwarf, is accompanied by her maid.
The picture was painted in Florence *c.* 1760 and is said to commemorate a visit which the Duke paid to Miss Mendes, with the intention of proposing marriage.
There is a portrait caricature of the Duke of Roxburghe by Patch in the National Portrait Gallery.
Former collection: Ampthill Park.
Coll.: *Mary, Countess of Ilchester, Holland House, London.*

90. A GROUP IN FLORENCE.
Oil, 28½×42 inches.

The group of eleven people includes the third Duke of Roxburghe seated in the centre, at back of him Mr. Wilbraham with raised hands, talking to Thomas Patch; Sir John Dick is playing the harpsichord and on the extreme right John Zoffany is showing a drawing to the

Hon. Felton Hervey. The painting on the wall is identical with the 'View of the Arno,' now in the collection of Mary, Countess of Ilchester.

Coll.: *The Duchess of Roxburghe, London.*

UNIDENTIFIED ARTIST

(Second Half of the Eighteenth Century)

91. CARICATURE GROUP OF IRISH GENTLEMEN.

Oil, 31×41 inches.

A note by Bishop John Leslie (born in 1772), preserved at Glaslough, gives the names of the characters in the picture, which are from left to right:

Kean O'Hara (1712–1782), dramatist and musician; Garret Wellesley, first Earl of Mornington (1735–1781), composer and professor of Music at Trinity College, Dublin—the father of the Duke of Wellington, the Marquess Wellesley, Lord Maryborough and Lord Cowley; General William Gardiner, younger brother of Luke, first Viscount Mountjoy; Mr. Meredyth, probably Henry Meredyth, of Broadstone, Dublin, Corrector of the Press and M.P. for Armagh from 1776 until his death in 1789; Mr. Fortescue, probably Thomas Fortescue, of Dromiskin, Co. Louth, a nephew of Lord Mornington, who died in 1780; John Prendergast Smyth, who was created Viscount Gort in 1816 and died in 1817; Richard Townsend, of Castle Townsend, Co. Cork; Sackville Gardiner (died 1796), an uncle of General William Gardiner, whose name is associated with the development of Sackville Street, Dublin; Charles Powell Leslie, of Glaslough, Co. Monaghan, a brother-in-law of Lord Mornington, who died in 1800 and at whose house, either in Dublin or at Glaslough, according to family tradition, the depicted party took place.

The painting has been variously attributed to Hogarth and to Reynolds. But as there is historical evidence to show that it was executed some time between 1769 and 1779, it cannot be by either of these artists, for Hogarth died in 1764 and Reynolds is known to have given up doing caricatures, which he considered beneath his dignity, in 1752. Mr. Strickland suggests that the picture might be by John Trotter, a contemporary Irish artist, who died in 1792.

Coll.: *Sir John and Lady Leslie, Glaslough, Co. Monaghan.*

WRIGHT OF DERBY, JOSEPH, A.R.A.

(1734–1797)

92. WILLIAM ERNES, ESQ. OF BOWBRIDGE, DERBYSHIRE, AND HIS FRIEND MR. TURNER.

Oil, 28×36½ inches.

The names of the artist and the gentlemen portrayed are inscribed on the back of the canvas.

Coll.: *Major V. H. Seymer, D.S.O., M.C., Worpledon, Surrey.*

WILSON, RICHARD, R.A.

(1714–1782)

93. GEORGE III AND HIS BROTHER, EDWARD AUGUSTUS, DUKE OF YORK AND ALBANY, AS CHILDREN.

Oil, 56×62 inches.

Painted in 1749.

Coll.: *The National Portrait Gallery, London.*

DANCE, NATHANIEL, R.A.
(1734–1811)

94. HUGH, SECOND DUKE OF NORTHUMBERLAND, AND MR. LIPPYAT.
Oil, 37¼×27½ inches.

Sir Hugh Percy, second Duke of Northumberland (1742–1817), became M.P. for Westminster in 1763 (until 1776).

Signed and dated: '*N. Dance f.* 1762.' As Dance left Rome and returned to England before 1761, the picture was probably painted in London and the Roman setting, with the Coliseum in the background, was introduced as a souvenir of the sitters' 'grand tour' to the Continent.

Coll.: *The Duke of Northumberland, Syon House.*

COTES, FRANCIS, R.A.
(1726–1770)

95. QUEEN CHARLOTTE WITH THE PRINCESS ROYAL AND THE DUCHESS OF ANCASTER.
Pen and wash drawing, 9½×6¾ inches.

A painting of the Queen with the Princess Royal in identical attitude, but without the figure of the Duchess of Ancaster, is in the Royal Collection at Windsor.

Coll.: *The British Museum.*

SANDBY, PAUL, R.A.
(1725–1809)

96. THREE DAUGHTERS OF THE SECOND EARL WALDEGRAVE WITH MISS KEPPEL, DAUGHTER OF THE BISHOP OF EXETER.
Water colour drawing, 4¾×6⅞ inches.

The three children on the left are Elisabeth Laura, afterwards Countess Waldegrave (died 1816); Charlotte Maria, afterwards Duchess of Grafton (died 1808); and Anne Horatia, afterwards Lady Hugh Seymour (died 1801). They were grand-nieces of Horace Walpole. The drawing was made at Windsor about 1769.

Coll.: *Victoria and Albert Museum, London.*

ATTRIBUTED TO ZOFFANY, JOHN, R.A.
(1733–1810)

97. A FAMILY GROUP.
Pencil drawing, 18×23 inches.

Coll.: *Thomas E. Lowinsky, Esq., London.*

COPLEY, JOHN SINGLETON, R.A.
(1737–1815)

98. THE SITWELL FAMILY.
Oil, 63×73 inches.

The children of Francis Hurt Sitwell (died 1793): The youth on the right is Sitwell Sitwell (1769–1811), who later became first Baronet; the younger boys are Francis (died 1813) and Hurt (died 1803); the girl is Mary, who married Sir Charles Wake in 1790 and died in childbirth a year later.

Painted in 1787.

Coll.: *Captain Osbert Sitwell, Renishaw Hall, Derbyshire.*

NASMYTH, ALEXANDER
(1758–1840)

99. LIEUT.-COLONEL JAMES EDMONSTOUN OF NEWTOUN AND JAMES VEITCH, LORD ELIOCK.
Oil, 44×60 inches.

Lord Eliock (1712–1793), Scottish judge, was a great favourite of Frederick the Great, whom he visited shortly after 1738 and with whom he later kept up a long correspondence.
Coll.: *The Marquess of Bute.*

DOWNMAN, JOHN, A.R.A.
(c. 1750–1824)

100. SIR RALPH ABERCROMBY AND HIS SECRETARY OR SON.
Oil, 30×25 inches.

Sir Ralph Abercromby (1734–1801) commanded in 1795–1796 the expedition against the French in the West Indies. This is recorded in the picture by a 'Plan of the Town and Bay of St. George in Grenada' on the table and a 'Map of the Island of Carriacon' which hangs on the wall.
Coll.: *The National Gallery, London.*

101. THE LARKIN FAMILY.
Water colour drawing, 28×41½ inches.

The drawing represents the family of John Larkin of Clare House, Malling: his wife Dorothy, daughter of Sir Charles Style, Bart., and his children—Lambert, Emily, Fanny, Camilla, Isabella, Caroline, John and Charles.
Executed *c.* 1806.
Coll.: *The Pierpont Morgan Collection.*

REINAGLE, PHILIP, R.A.
(1749–1833)

102. MR. JAMES SETON, OF TOUCH HOUSE, WITH HIS HORSE, ACCOMPANIED BY AN INDIAN SERVANT.
Oil, 39½×30 inches.

From the collection of Sir Douglas Seton Stewart, Bart., of Touch House, Stirling.
Coll.: *Sir Herbert Hughes-Stanton, R.A., London.*

MORTIMER, JOHN HAMILTON, A.R.A.
(1741–1789) .

103. THE TYRWHITT-DRAKE FAMILY AT SHARDELOES.
Oil, 67×91 inches.

Members of the Tyrwhitt-Drake family at Shardeloes, near Amersham, Buckinghamshire. Shardeloes, originally built by Wyatt, was completed and decorated by the brothers Adam during 1759–1761, and it has been suggested that the two men standing on the right are their portrayals. There appears to be no evidence to support this suggestion.
Coll.: *Captain Thomas Tyrwhitt-Drake, M.C., J.P., Shardeloes, Bucks.*

RIGAUD, J. F., R.A.
(1742–1810)

104. THE LOCKER FAMILY.
  Oil, 40×63 inches.

On the back of the canvas is the following inscription by the late Frederick Locker-Lampson: 'This picture was painted for my Grandfather Captain W. Locker by Rigaud about 1779. It represents my Grandfather and Grandmother, their eldest daughter Lucy who died a nun in Bruges, Wm. Locker afterwards in the Army, John Locker who had a good appointment at Malta and died there, Eliza (with the dog Argus) an excellent woman, who died unmarried in Liverpool, and my father, Edward Hawke, in his mother's lap. Eliza was so short that as I have heard my Father say when she could walk she could walk under the dining table. F. Locker, May 1870.'

Captain William Locker (1731–1800) had a distinguished career in the navy. He married in 1770 Lucy, daughter of Admiral William Parry. Edward Hawke Locker (1777–1849) became commissioner of Greenwich Hospital, where he originally started the picture gallery in 1823.

Coll.: *Arthur de Casseres, Esq., London.*

IBBETSON, JULIUS CAESAR
(1759–1819)

105. VIEW OF THE INTERIOR OF THE KEEP AT CARDIFF CASTLE.
  Oil, 26×35 inches.

The Keep is depicted as it stood in 1800, having been 'slighted' during the Civil War by Cromwell's cannon. The figures include, besides most of the Cardiff notabilities of the day, John, Marquess of Bute, and John, Viscount Mountstewart, who form the centre of the right-hand group. In the centre of the picture stand 'Old Frankie,' Keeper of the Cardiff Town Hall, then aged 94, and William Morgan, the Porter, who holds the Castle Mace, still used at official functions.

Coll.: *The Marquess of Bute.*

EDRIDGE, HENRY, A.R.A.
(1769–1821)

106. A GENTLEMAN AND TWO CHILDREN.
  Water colour and pencil drawing, 12½×9¼ inches.

Signed and dated 1799.
Coll.: *Victoria and Albert Museum, London.*

WHEATLEY, FRANCIS, R.A.
(1747–1801)

107. RALPH WINSTANLEY WOOD AND HIS SON, WILLIAM WARREN.

108. MRS. RALPH WINSTANLEY WOOD AND HER TWO DAUGHTERS.
  Companion pieces, oils, each 28×35 inches.

Ralph Winstanley Wood (1745–1831), son of William Winstanley Wood, of Wigan, Lancs., had an army career before his friend Warren Hastings persuaded him to become a salt agent. He married Mary Margaretta Pearce (1746–1808) and in 1785 purchased Pierrepont

Place, Frensham, Surrey, which later passed to Crawford Davison, who married Wood's daughter, Mary.

The portrait of Mrs. Wood is signed with initials, *F. W.*

From the collection of Major John Winstanley Cobb, a descendant of the Wood family.

Coll.: *The Knoedler Galleries.*

109. THE EARL OF CARLISLE IN PHOENIX PARK, DUBLIN.
    Oil.

Frederick Howard, fifth Earl of Carlisle (1748–1825), who was Lord Lieutenant of Ireland from 1780 to 1782, is here seen surrounded by his family and members of the viceregal household.

Painted in Ireland.

Coll.: *The Earl of Carlisle, Castle Howard.*

TURNER, JOSEPH MALLORD WILLIAM, R.A.

(1775-1851)

110. MUSICAL PARTY, PETWORTH.
    Oil, 48×35½ inches.

This unfinished sketch was probably painted about 1830, at the same time as the 'Interior at Petworth' in the National Gallery.

Coll.: *The National Gallery, Millbank.*

LESLIE, CHARLES ROBERT, R.A.

(1794-1859)

111. THE HOLLAND HOUSE LIBRARY.
    Oil, 22¼×29 inches.

Lord and Lady Holland with their librarian and secretary.

Painted for Lord Holland and bequeathed by Lady Holland to the second Earl Grey.

Coll.: *The Earl Grey, London.*

OAKLEY, OCTAVIUS

(1800-1867)

112. SIR RERESBY SITWELL AND HIS BROTHER AND SISTERS.
    Water colour drawing, 18×28 inches.

Sir Reresby Sitwell (1820–1862) was the third Baronet.

Painted about 1828.

Coll.: *Captain Osbert Sitwell, Renishaw Hall, Derbyshire.*

MARSHALL, BENJAMIN

(1767-1835)

113. THE WESTON FAMILY.
    Oil, 40×50 inches.

Painted in 1818.

Coll.: *G. D. Widener, Esq., Philadelphia, U.S.A.*

FERNELEY, JOHN
(1781–1860)

114. THE FERNELEY FAMILY.
>Oil, 41½×60⅞ inches.

From left to right: Miss Caroline Johnson, Ferneley's granddaughter who became Mrs. Norman; Mrs. Johnson (1812–1903), Ferneley's elder daughter; his son Claude Loraine Ferneley (1822–1892); John Ferneley, standing; his younger daughter, Mrs. Mason (1817–1886), whose daughter Polly, seated on a donkey, is next to Charles Allen Ferneley (1844–1931), the artist's son by his second wife.
>Painted about 1855.
>Coll.: *T. B. Yuille, Esq., New York.*

115. COUNT D'ORSAY ON HORSEBACK AT HYDE PARK CORNER.
>Oil, 34×42½ inches.

Count Alfred Guillaume Gabriel d'Orsay (1801–1852), the famous dandy, is seen on horseback near the newly erected statue of Achilles. The picture was painted during the early years of his connection with Lady Blessington, who then lived near by in Park Lane.
>Signed and dated: *J. Ferneley, Melton Mowbray,* 1823.
>Formerly in the collection of D. H. Farr, Esq., New York.
>Coll.: *The Tooth Galleries.*

116. JOHN FERNELEY AND HIS DAUGHTER ON HORSEBACK.
>Oil, 21¼×33½ inches.
>Coll.: *Private ownership, America.*

THORBURN, ROBERT, A.R.A.
(1818–1885)

117. THE DUKE OF WELLINGTON WITH THE CHILDREN OF LORD CHARLES WELLESLEY AT STRATHFIELDSAYE.
>Painted on ivory, 17½×26 inches.

The Duke of Wellington is seen with his four grandchildren, who are from left to right: Henry (later third Duke), Mary (later Lady Mary Scott), Arthur (later fourth Duke) and Victoria (later Lady Holm Patrick).

The picture was executed at Conholt Park, Andover, in the early summer of 1852, a few months before the Duke's death. The background was put in after the figures were painted and represents the library at Strathfieldsaye.

Painted for the Baroness Burdett-Coutts and bought by the present owner at her sale in 1922.
>Coll.: *Lord Gerald Wellesley, London.*

CONSTABLE, JOHN, R.A.
(1776–1837)

118. ALEXANDER POPE AND HIS FAMILY.
>Oil.

On the left Alexander Pope (1763–1835), actor and painter, is seen with his two younger sons and their tutor. His elder son is on the right next to a lady who has been identified from a portrait by Shee at the Garrick Club as Pope's second wife—Marie Ann Pope (1775–1803), the actress.

According to Sir Charles Holmes 'the date of Mrs. Pope's death shows that the picture must have been started in 1803. But the work is more refined and accomplished than Constable's other products of that time, so we must assume that the group was not finished until three or four years later. Had it not been for the agreement of family tradition with the portrait at the Garrick Club, I should have made the date 1807–1808, and supposed the lady to be Pope's third wife, the widow of Francis Wheatley, R.A.'

We have been unable to ascertain the present ownership of the picture.

HUMPHRY, OZIAS, R.A.
(1742–1810)

119. THE HEYGATE FAMILY.
   Oil, 74×50 inches.

The three children of the banker, James Heygate of Aldermanbury, London, Hackney, Middlesex, and Southend, Essex: William (1782–1844) in the centre, his brother James (1784–1873) sketching, and their sister Elizabeth Anne.

William Heygate became M.P. for Sudbury, an alderman of the City of London, Lord Mayor in 1822–1823, and was created a Baronet in 1831.

The picture was painted about 1800 at 13 Old Bond Street, where Humphry had his studio.

From the collection of Major W. H. Heygate, Roecliff Manor, Loughborough.

Coll.: *The Leger Galleries*.

CARPENTER, MARGARET SARAH
(1793–1872)

120. THE HICKS CHILDREN.
   Oil, 31½×26½ inches.

Coll.: *The Leger Galleries*.

PARTRIDGE, JOHN
(1790–1872)

121. SIR GEORGE SITWELL AND HIS FAMILY.
   Oil, 75×59 inches.

Sir George Sitwell, second Baronet (1797–1853), married in 1818 Susan, eldest daughter of Craufurd Tait of Harviestoun, Co. Clackmannan.

Painted about 1828.

Coll.: *Capt. Osbert Sitwell, Renishaw Hall, Derbyshire*.

DENNING, STEPHEN POYNTZ
(1795–1864)

122. THE CHILDREN OF ELHANAN BIRKNELL, ESQ.
   Water colour drawing.

Signed and dated 1841.
Exhibited at the Royal Academy in 1842.
Coll.: *Victoria and Albert Museum, London*.

STONE, FRANK, A.R.A.

(1800–1859)

123. SAMUEL ROGERS, HON. MRS. CAROLINE NORTON AND MRS. PHIPPS.
Oil, 24×29 inches.

Samuel Rogers (1763–1855), the banker-poet, is seen with Mrs. Norton, afterwards Lady Stirling-Maxwell (1808–1877), the poetess, on the right and Mrs. Phipps on the left.
The picture, which is unfinished, was painted about 1850.
Coll.: *The National Portrait Gallery, London.*

BARRAUD, WILLIAM (1810–1850), AND HENRY (1812–1874)

124. THE BEAUFORT HUNT LAWN MEET AT BADMINTON.
Oil, 80½×116¼ inches.

Henry, seventh Duke of Beaufort (1792–1853), in foreground, on horseback.
Painted in 1836. Henry Barraud did the figures and William the scenery.
Coll.: *The Hon. Mrs. Macdonald-Buchanan, Lavington Park, Sussex.*

UNIDENTIFIED ARTIST

(c. 1840)

125. VICTORIAN INTERIOR.
Oil, 28×36 inches.
Coll.: *Oliver Brown, Esq., London.*

GRANT, SIR FRANCIS, P.R.A.

(1803–1878)

126. THE MELTON BREAKFAST.
Oil, 28½×38¼ inches.

The group represents from left to right: Massey Stanley, the Earl of Wilton, Count Matuscewitz, Lord Gardner, Walter Little Gilmour, Lyne Stephens, the Club servant, Sir Frederick Johnstone, Lord Rokeby, Lord Forester, Lord Kinnaird and Sir Rowland Errington, Master of the Quorn from 1835 to 1838, to whom the picture was presented on his retirement.
On the walls hang two paintings by Ferneley and a map of Leicestershire.
A replica with two additional figures is in the collection of the Duke of Rutland.
Exhibited at the Royal Academy in 1834.
Coll.: *Lord Cromer, London.*

127. QUEEN VICTORIA RIDING OUT AT WINDSOR CASTLE.
Oil, 38×53 inches.

By the side of the Queen is Lord Melbourne; in the foreground the Marquess Conyngham; under the archway the Earl of Uxbridge, the Hon. George Byng, Sir G. Quintin and Miss Quintin. In front are the Queen's two dogs, Isley and Dash.
Painted in 1839. Exhibited at the Royal Academy in 1840.
Coll.: *His Majesty the King, Windsor.*

WINTERHALTER, FRANZ XAVER
(1806–1873)

128. THE DUKE OF WELLINGTON PRESENTING A CASKET ON PRINCE ARTHUR'S BIRTHDAY.
Oil, 42¼ × 51 inches.

Queen Victoria, escorted by the Prince Consort, is holding up Prince Arthur, the present Duke of Connaught (born 1st May 1850), to whom the aged Duke of Wellington, who died in 1852, is presenting a casket.

Coll.: *His Majesty the King, Windsor.*

BARKER, J. J.

129. SHOOTING PARTY AT SANDRINGHAM, 1867.
Oil, 43⅓ × 61½ inches.

The personages represented are from left to right: Major Teesdale, V.C., Lord Aveland (afterwards Earl of Ancaster), Lord Londesborough, the Duke of Beaufort, Major-General Sir Arthur Ellis, the Duke of St. Albans, H.R.H. the Prince of Wales (afterwards King Edward VII), Mr. Christopher Sykes, the Earl of Chesterfield and Lord Huntingfield.

A companion picture to the above represents a *Shooting Party at Gisburne Park, Yorkshire,* and includes portraits of Prince Francis of Teck, Lord Londesborough, the Earl of Tankerville, etc.

From the collection of the Marquess of Lincolnshire, Dawes Hall, High Wycombe.

Coll.: *The Leger Galleries.*

WELLS, HENRY TANWORTH, R.A.
(1828–1903)

130. A PORTRAIT GROUP.
Oil, 49¼ × 63½ inches.

Seated from left to right are: George P. Boyce, Joanna Mary Wells (*née* Boyce) and Henry T. Wells. Standing at the back is John R. Clayton.

Joanna Mary Boyce (1831–1861) was a painter, and a retrospective exhibition of her work was held at the Tate Gallery in 1935. Her head and hands in the picture were painted a fortnight before her death.

Exhibited at the Royal Academy in 1862 under the title 'Portraits—including the portrait of the late Mrs. Wells.'

Coll.: *Mrs. Street, Bath.*

INDEX

(The Names of Persons portrayed are not given separately when specified under the Artists' Names. The 'Notes on the Illustrations' have not been indexed. Numerals in italic type refer to the *figure numbers* of illustrations.)

INDEX